The Paddler's
Guide to Michigan

The Paddler's Guide to Michigan

Jeff Counts

First Edition

THE COUNTRYMAN PRESS
WOODSTOCK, VERMONT

With time, access points may change—and road numbers, signs, and landmarks referred to in this book may be altered. If you find that such changes have occurred near the streams described in this book, please let the author and publisher know, so that corrections may be made in future editions. Other comments and suggestions are also welcome.

Library of Congress Cataloging-in-Publication Data has been applied for
The Paddler's Guide to Michigan
ISBN 978–0–88150–930–4

Interior photographs by the author unless otherwise specified
Maps by Paul Woodward © The Countryman Press

Book design and composition by Faith Hague

Published by The Countryman Press, P.O. Box 748, Woodstock, VT 05091

Distributed by W. W. Norton & Company, Inc., 500 Fifth Avenue, New York, NY 10110

Printed in the United States of America

10 9 8 7 6 5 4 3 2 1

Contents

Introduction

Most paddling guides do little more than dump paddlers in a river or lake and tell them where to get out. This guide does more. It gives readers the experience of being on the water and offers paddling times, along with offering opinionated suggestions on where to stay and eat.

This guide covers the recreational paddler's lifestyle by providing information on how to best see Michigan's more than 3,000 miles of Great Lakes coastline, inland lakes, and thousands of miles of rivers. It takes recreational paddlers to the best places, but even extreme sports folks may find new waters in this guide.

I've divided the guide into geographical sections so paddlers can see all the paddling opportunities available in a region at a glance to help better plan trips. I've included camping spots on lakes or rivers that will appeal to paddlers.

If there's any state best seen from a canoe or kayak, it's Michigan. Its history and geography are defined by water. The first explorers were French Canadian fur trappers and priests who made the long trek from Montreal in canoes. The state's two peninsulas were separated by the lakes until joined by the Mackinac Bridge about 50 years ago.

Where do you start? You can put a canoe or kayak in almost

Launching a boat

anywhere and have a decent time. This guide takes paddlers to the best water with the best scenery. I've included paddling itineraries for those planning trips. These are designed to give paddlers with limited time an overall view of a region and the diverse waters that can be found.

As the author of *Michigan: An Explorer's Guide,* I've designed this paddling book to work hand-in-glove with the Michigan guide and with *Trout Streams of Michigan,* another Countryman Press book.

The Countryman Press has a tradition of allowing its authors to be honest, and I have kept up that mantle of responsibility. The material put out by state Web sites and chambers of commerce makes things look rosy all the time. They aren't. From more than 30 years as a paddler and fly angler in Michigan, I know the bug season and the weather—and have striven to put guide users on the water at the best possible times.

This guide introduces you to a network of paddling guides, fly-fishing shop owners, and others who know Michigan's waters. Some are trusted friends; others have long-held reputations for guiding and out-fitting paddlers. I've included telephone numbers and Web sites, please feel free to contact them.

The times are changing in the kayaking world, and I've reflected that in this guide. There are more outfitters these days—some offering adventure trips to Isle Royale and the Apostle Islands, and others who offer wine tours and food tours in the Grand Traverse region. There's also the Antrim County Chain of Lakes tour that takes paddlers to B&Bs and upscale restaurants along the way.

This guide is Internet savvy and is the only paddling guide to Michigan that lists outfitters, canoe/kayak liveries, and government agencies that maintain Web sites with river and lake information. If you have a question that the book doesn't answer, check the Web sites listed. And although this isn't a technical book, I've included tips about gear, bug repellent, a discussion about canoes versus kayaks, and river ethics.

Unfortunately, a few of the state's rivers receive the most paddling traffic, and this book is aimed at helping paddlers find quieter waters. These rivers often don't have canoe liveries, but I've done my best to find vehicle spotting services (services that pick up and drop off your vehicle where you're going to or getting out of the river) in the more remote areas. A stop at a local gas station often yields information about a reliable person who can spot your vehicle.

I've also adjusted many of the paddling times in this guide, using higher numbers than usually given. This is based on my experience with them, which has been frustrating at times. Most paddling times used by government agencies, outfitters, and canoe/kayak liveries are based on how long it takes if you're doing nothing but paddling. That tends to push paddlers to be in a hurry—which is what liveries want you to do, so their shuttles can run efficiently. You're out there to have a good time and enjoy the scenery or the water, so there shouldn't be any rush. Since I often fish when I paddle, I just about double my time. My time estimates build in some time for sightseeing and taking breaks, so don't be surprised that you get to a place earlier than expected— especially if you're a hard-core paddler.

As for time on the water, I'd plan four-hour trips. For recreational paddlers that's about enough time in a canoe or kayak for one day. I've gone longer—much longer—and regretted it the next day.

In the back of the guide, there's a section called "Rivers Noted." These are waters that can be paddled, but which I couldn't recommend to recreational paddlers either because of their difficulty or simply because they aren't very scenic. Environmental factors have also been taken into consideration. Michigan is a very industrialized state and I don't want to put you on contaminated waters.

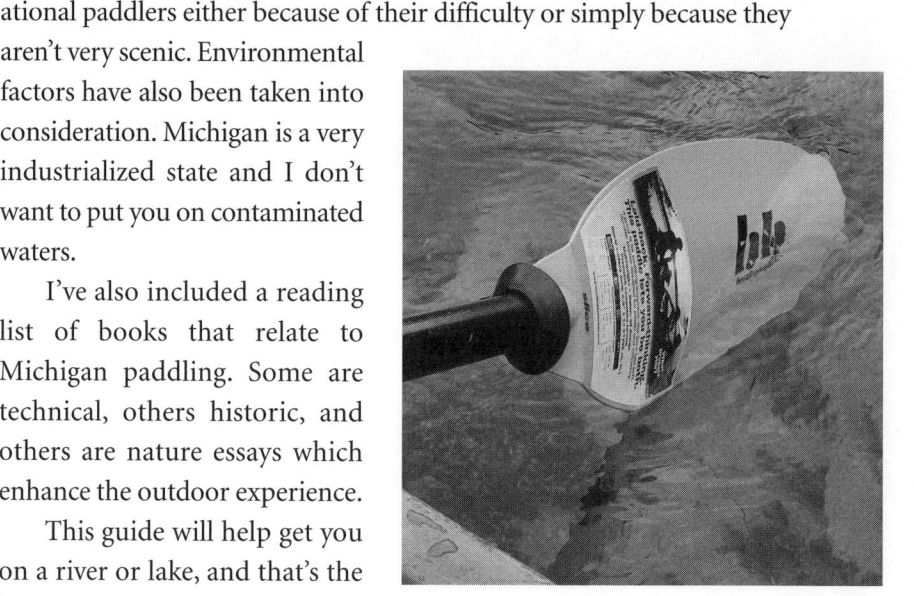

I've also included a reading list of books that relate to Michigan paddling. Some are technical, others historic, and others are nature essays which enhance the outdoor experience.

This guide will help get you on a river or lake, and that's the best way to see Michigan.

There are many strokes during a trip

How to Use This Book

THERE'S A SHORT DESCRIPTION of what waters there are at the beginning of each geographic section, along with a suggested paddling itinerary that's intended to show paddlers the various opportunities. When called for, there is a summary at the top of each chapter on a body of water that's designed to help the paddler make a quick decision as to whether they want to try that river or lake.

At the end of each geographic section, I've included suggestions on lodging and eating out that I think will appeal to paddlers. If you're looking for more extensive listings, please pick up my other Countryman Press book, *Michigan: An Explorer's Guide.*

A paddler prepares to lift his kayak over a log

Paddling Terms

I've tried to keep this guide free of jargon, but there are a few terms that I just couldn't get around. Here they are:

- *Put-in.* It's the place on the river where you put in your canoe or kayak.
- *Take-out.* Where you take your boat out.
- *Lift over.* You'll get this one the first time you're required to do it. You have to get out of the watercraft and into the water and lift your boat over an obstruction, usually a log across a river.

Skills Needed

The paddling sports are fairly intuitive, but what's easy for one person is often difficult for another. I've included the paddling skills needed for the various bodies of water included in the guide, but they are a general indication of what you'll need to know. I'd suggest that paddlers take a lesson (or at least read an instructional book) before a first trip. For information on classes and books, go to www.americancanoe.org.

Beginner: A paddler with basic skills who can steer on a river and knows basic water safety.

Intermediate: A person who has mastered the ability to maneuver a watercraft, and knows self-rescue techniques and can help others.

Advanced: Experts with the ability to handle most river and lake conditions and who know how to rescue others.

Canoes versus Kayaks

THIS GUIDE IS DESIGNED for recreational paddlers seeking to get involved in recreational canoeing/kayaking and who are looking for pleasant outdoor experiences. It's based on my 30 years of mistakes; I've made them, so you don't.

The first thing to decide is a canoe versus a kayak. I like the versatility of a canoe, you can fish out of it, use it for camping, and two people can have a lot of fun in it. I've had my Old Towne for about 12 years, and while it has its share of dents and scrapes, it keeps on going. It's 17 feet and weights about 50 pounds, so I can easily hoist it on top of my Jeep by myself.

Since it's older, I don't much worry about it. When I first bought it, I read all the instructions and worried about what sort of damage the sun beating down on it would do. Those concerns didn't last. I figured if there was some damage over 30 or so years, it wouldn't be enough to worry about. I want equipment I can use, not just maintain.

Kayaking is a relatively newer sport in Michigan, and sales are booming. They are fun and easy to use in Michigan waters. With a good rack, you can carry two of them on the top of your vehicle.

But before you decide on which boat is right for you, try renting one of each and take an afternoon paddle. Check your local sporting goods retailer; many hold events where paddlers can try different boats. There are also all sorts of styles and shapes for both canoes and kayaks; you'll just have to decide which is right for you.

If you're planning on getting out on the Great Lakes, a 15- to 17-foot sea kayak is required for safety. I've seen people on the big lakes with small river kayaks and sit-on-top-type boats, none of which are adequate to handle the rough seas, which in the Great Lakes can come up quickly. Getting into sea kayaking also requires some education, including self-rescue techniques. I've listed outfitters who offer lessons and tours of the Great Lakes.

If I was on a limited budget and wanted to seriously get involved in the paddling sports, I'd buy a lightweight canoe as my first boat. They're easy to get in and out of and you can take a companion with you.

My first trip would be to the bookstore, not the river, for a copy of Bill Mason's *Song of the Paddle.* I think it's the best instructional book. Mason's tips are based on his many canoe trips through the Canadian wilderness. He covers the various paddles, strokes, and paddling alone. It drives me nuts when I see images of lone paddlers in still lakes sitting in the back of the canoe. It may be idyllic looking, but it's the wrong place to be. When you paddle a canoe alone, you're supposed to turn the boat around and sit it the bow seat. It may look funny, but you're supposed to paddle the boat backward. The reason is that you want as much of the boat's bottom making contact with the water as possible; this is for stability. When you're sitting in the bow seat, you're closer to the middle of the boat and have that stability.

After digesting a bit of Bill Mason, head for a nearby pond or small lake on a calm day and start practicing. Early morning or evenings are

A kayak and canoe ready for adventure

Quiet waters and time for reflection

good times of day, when the winds die down. Practice getting in and out of the boat, and just remember one thing—stay low and keep your weight in the middle of the canoe.

If you're new to kayaking, my first stop would again be the bookstore for a copy of Ken Whiting's *Recreational Kayaking: The Ultimate Guide.* The book is packed with pictures and simple text that will get you into the sport on a recreational basis—and includes boat handing, paddling, and gear. Then I'd head to a small, calm lake.

Those outings on placid water will pay off when you try your first swift river, where you're going to be required to do some fancy paddlework to avoid getting dumped in the water. When you think you're ready, head for an easy river first. I've included an upcoming section in this book entitled First Rivers, which are recommended for beginners because of their ease of paddling.

Just a note on Michigan rivers. There is very little whitewater in Michigan, so it's a great place for recreational paddling, but there are some rivers with tight turns that require some expertise.

Gear

WE'RE LIVING IN an age of stuff. When I first started paddling in the 1970s, you pretty much just wore whatever old clothing you had. Those were the bad old days. We now have much better clothing that dries quickly and some of which is nearly waterproof. One quick tip—don't ever wear jeans for paddling. Wearing a pair of wet, heavy jeans can spoil an outing.

But where to start? I'd suggest the L. L. Bean catalog as a first step. It features clothing, canoes/kayaks, and related gear that will give you some idea of what you need. REI also offers comparable clothing and gear, and they have stores and an online presence.

But before you spend too much, here's a list of essentials:

- *A personal flotation device (PFD)* is required by every person in the boat, and it should be worn at all times. Make sure it fits properly. Several people drown annually even in shallow Michigan rivers.
- *Quick-drying clothing and underwear.* Some of the stuff they have now is unbelievable. You can be drenched and simply take the stuff off, wring it out, shake it in the air, and it's nearly dry. Again, don't wear jeans or sweatshirts, or even take them with you—they're useless when wet.
- *A rain parka, even on nice-looking days.* I like Gore-Tex the best. Mine is about 12 years old, and still looks brand new even after rough use. It's from L. L. Bean. A parka doesn't only keep off the rain; if you tend to get cold, it also gives you a layer of warmth.
- *A fleece vest or jacket.* They are easily stuffed into a small bag, and can be put on in case you go into the river and get cold.

- *Sandals.* The sport ones are the best because they're lightweight and cover much of the foot, which is great when walking on rocky surfaces. If you tend to get cold, add a pair of wool socks or neoprene booties.
- *A hat.* Baseball caps are all the fashion, but a floppy hat that protects the ears from the sun is more practical. I use an old, felt, brimmed floppy hat. On hot days, I dip it into the river, get it wet, and provide my own air-conditioning.
- *A small pack to carry your lunch, water, parka, fleece, and other gear.* They need not be expensive for just an afternoon trip—but if you know you're going to be doing a lot of paddling, a dry bag is a good investment. They can be sealed and are water-tight. For cell phones and cameras, they sell sealable plastic pouches. But don't forget about plastic zip-lock bags from your kitchen—they're cheaper and handy. I take several of them in case of emergency. If you really want to be prepared for an emergency night in the woods, pack a couple of large garbage bags—they provide instant, cheap shelter from the rain, cold, and insects.
- *GPS or a compass.* Take both. GPS fans will find they don't always work in Michigan's backcountry, so a compass is a good backup. Even if you're on a river (where there is little chance of getting lost) at least take a compass in case of an emergency that requires you to find the nearest road quickly.

Top Paddling Destinations

Rivers

- *Pere Marquette, near Baldwin, Lower Peninsula.* While many Michigan rivers are really a series of rivers separated by dams, the Pere Marquette flows freely through much of its course, allowing you to see the way rivers acted in the past.
- *Au Sable, the big waters at Mio, Lower Peninsula.* This is a lovely river that shouldn't be missed; it's spring-fed and doesn't get low during the summer. It's crowded near Grayling, but the river is wider at Mio—and there are fewer people.

Inland Lakes

- *Beaver Lakes, Pictured Rocks National Lake Shore, Upper Peninsula.* A pure paddling lake, with few motorboats and no shoreline development. A small stream runs from it to Lake Superior.
- *Sable Lake, Grand Marais, Upper Peninsula.* An undeveloped shoreline, views of the dunes, and little motorboat traffic.

Great Lakes

- *Keweenaw Peninsula, Lake Superior, Upper Peninsula.* The peninsula provides tremendous access to the lake, and there are many protected harbors and bays to paddle.
- *Pictured Rocks National Lakeshore, Lake Superior, Upper Peninsula.* The rocks and arches are iconic views of Michigan.
- *Sleeping Bear Dunes National Lakeshore, Lake Michigan, Lower Peninsula.* Miles of parkland shoreline with stunning views of the dunes.

First Rivers

W<small>HEN</small> I F<small>IRST</small> started talking to people about doing a paddling guide for Michigan, I received a great e-mail from a woman who had just taken her two teenage children on a paddling trip. She used the term *first rivers,* and I owe this chapter to her.

She made a good point. Many outdoor people gain their skills over the years, and have a foundation (and gear) of skills from which to start on a new pursuit. I started out as a hippie backpacker in the early 1970s and moved on to long-distance bicycling, fly-fishing, upland bird hunting, and paddling. Skills from each pursuit followed me to the next.

Getting into a canoe or kayak for the first time, especially with two teenagers, can take some courage. You don't want to end up on some wild river, on a seemingly endless trip. Before you go, here are some tips. Don't let anybody wear jeans or sweatshirts; they soak up the water quickly, and you're going to be miserable the remainder of the day. Wear a hat that covers your ears, it can keep sunstroke and dehydration at bay. Bring water, never beer. Alcohol leads to dehydration. Save the beer for around the campfire at night.

Here's a list of First Rivers that are easy for a first time paddler and that are covered in this book:

- Platte River
- Muskegon
- The Au Sable, from Mio downriver
- Huron River near Ann Arbor, a mostly slow moving stream, and close to home for many
- Au Train River, central Upper Peninsula, a short ride for kids

Paddling History of Michigan

Wᴴɪʟᴇ sɪᴛᴛɪɴɢ ɪɴ a $2,000 molded plastic sea kayak in Lake Superior, it's difficult to envision the paddling heritage of Michigan and the surrounding Great Lakes state. As you paddle along the Pictured Rocks or the sandy coastline, it's difficult to imagine that you're not the first person to visit there.

While making a difficult paddle in high waves, I can't imagine how it was for Native American paddlers who braved the lakes for a thousand years in flimsy birch-bark canoes or how it was for the French Canadian voyageurs who paddled at a required 55 strokes per minute (try it sometime) and carried 90-pound packs on portages.

These days we don't have to stop along the way and patch a birch-bark canoe. Rarely do our plastic boats need repair. While the Native Americans and French Canadians tried to stay warm using buckskin clothing, wool blankets, and canvas, we are almost insulated from our experience by fleece as well as quick drying, almost waterproof clothing. And at the end of the day, if we're camping, there's the reassuring hiss of a gas stove warming our food.

On nights like that, I think about the French Canadians who were huddled wet and cold next to a fire eating pea soup or some other basic foods. Perhaps there was some brandy at the end of their 14-hour day.

In a way, all of our modern outdoor pursuits and accomplishments are due to technology. Up until after World War II, with the advent of aluminum canoes, most craft were canvas and required a lot of maintenance. The aluminum (and later fiberglass) canoes were heavy and difficult to portage. Thanks to modern chemistry, the new generation of canoes (and now kayaks) are much lighter, easier to portage, and

A canoe put up for the night

need little maintenance. In a way, these new watercraft are closer to their birch-bark ancestors, because they're lighter in weight.

We're living in the golden age of paddling.

The settling of the Great Lakes region is intertwined with paddling. The French from their bases in Montreal and Quebec quickly adopted the Native American birch-bark canoe as the best mode of travel through the lakes, and the simple craft opened up the fur trade.

Beaver skin hats were all the rage in Europe during the 17th and 18th centuries, and the French were able to profit from that market by making forays into the Great Lakes region in large cargo canoes filled with trade goods for Native Americans.

Mackinac Island, which is a tourist destination in northern Lake Huron, was once a hub for the fur trade. It's where John Jacob Astor, America's first millionaire, made his fortune with his American Fur Company.

But it was the French, not the English or Americans, who engaged in the first explorations. Many place names in the region bear French names—Detroit, Marquette, and Sault Saint Marie being just a few.

Louis Jolliet and Jacques Marquette were two French explorers who established French dominance in the Great Lakes, the Mississippi River, and throughout much of the West. Jolliet was a fur trader and Marquette a Jesuit priest. In 1673 they and five others headed west in canoes along the cost of Lake Michigan from St. Ignace on an expedition to the Mississippi River. They followed the lakeshore to Green Bay, and paddled the Fox River to the Mississippi River following it downstream as far as the Arkansas River.

When they noticed Native Americans sporting Spanish trade goods, they headed northward—worried they would be captured by the Spanish. Jolliet eventually returned to French Canada, but Marquette died of dysentery on his return trip and is thought to be buried somewhere on the Lake Michigan coast.

However, Jolliet and Marquette weren't the first Frenchmen to arrive in Green Bay via a canoe. The flamboyant Thomas Nicolette, who traded with the Native Americans, paddled across Lake Michigan in 1634, becoming the first European to cross the lake. He was looking for a passage to China when he landed in Green Bay—and was wearing a colorful Chinese silk robe, thinking he was close to the Orient. He thought he would blend in with the natives, but instead stood out to the Native American tribes.

But the most colorful of the early Great Lakes paddlers were the Voyageurs, who were mostly French Canadian fur traders, who reached into every nook and cranny of the lakes region in search of furs. They would either trade for them with Native Americans or trap animals themselves. They were the tough lot required to paddle at 55 strokes a minute!

That heritage lives on today in Canada. The Au Sable River Canoe Marathon in late July in Grayling attracts French Canadians, and many times they are the top finishers in the annual event.

What's Where in Michigan

Airports and Airlines: There are seven major airports with regular commercial service. Metro Airport near Detroit is the major one and is a hub for Delta Airlines. Bishop Airport near Flint also serves southeast Michigan. Gerald R. Ford Airport near Grand Rapids has regular service. Midland-Bay City Saginaw and Lansing airports have major airline service, too, but most are connector flights to Detroit, Chicago, or Cleveland. Marquette's K. I. Sawyer Airport has the most service to the UP.

Area Codes: Starting in the Lower Peninsula, area codes are 313 (Detroit), 734 (western Wayne County and Ann Arbor), 248 and 810 (northern Oakland County), 269 (southwestern Michigan), 517 (central Michigan), 989 (northwestern Michigan, Saginaw Valley, the Thumb, and parts of northern Michigan), 231 (northwestern Michigan), and 906 (the entire Upper Peninsula [UP]).

Au Sable River Canoe Marathon: Held annually on the last full weekend of July, the canoe race attracts top canoe paddlers from the United States and Canada. The 120-mile route from Grayling to Oscoda is billed as the longest such nonstop race in North America. Thousands of spectators line the banks to watch the paddlers race through the night. The race starts at 9 PM, and Canadians usually dominate the race. Winning times are generally slightly over 14 hours. For more information, go to www.ausablecanoemarathon.org.

Books: One of the first books about paddling in Michigan was Henry Wadsworth Longfellow's Song of Hiawatha, an epic poem published in 1855. Although Longfellow never visited Michigan and relied mostly on nonfiction works published by Henry Rowe Schoolcraft, an early explorer, the poem did much to immortalize the vision of Native Americans gliding through North Woods waters in canoes. Although

Sigurd Olson (1899–1982) didn't write about Michigan, his canoeing and nature essays helped define the North Woods paddling experience. Start with *Reflections from the North Country* and then move on to his others—*The Singing Wilderness, The Lonely Land, Runes of the North,* and *Of Time and Place.* As for technical material, Ken Whiting has a decent, usable book out titled *Recreational Kayaking: The Ultimate Guide.* The book has many photos, and is good for a person just getting into kayaking. Bill Mason (1929–1988) was a passionate Canadian canoeist whose books, films, and documentaries helped define the sport. *Path of the Paddle* is his best on canoeing styles, and *Song of the Paddle* addresses wilderness canoe travel. Additionally, the guide books *Michigan: An Explorer's Guide* and *Great Destinations: The Upper Peninsula,* both from The Countryman Press, are good guides for getting around the state.

Camping: More than 3 million acres of federal and state forestlands are open to rustic, backwoods camping—which for paddlers means you can set up camp on any piece of public land, unless prohibited. That said, camping along many rivers and lakes can be difficult because there aren't always suitable spots. Before you decide to take a canoe/kayak

Canoe camping spots often have signs

camping trip check with federal or state forest officials. River maps with established campsites are often available. Canoe/kayak liveries also have maps and information about camping.

Fall Foliage: The colors start to change anywhere from mid-September in the UP to early October in southern Michigan. The first week of October can be the best for northern Michigan and the UP.

Hunting: Paddlers are most likely to encounter duck and geese hunters on Michigan waters. The wildfowl season starts in mid-September and runs through early winter. Most wildfowl hunters stick to small lakes and marshes and generally won't be found on rivers or the Great Lakes. Most wildfowl hunting takes place in the early morning hours around dawn, and in the evening near dusk. Small game season starts in mid-September and runs through mid-November, when the rifle deer season starts. By mid-November, the weather has turned cold enough so that paddling is uncomfortable.

Lighthouses: There are 115 lighthouses on the four Great Lakes surrounding Michigan. Some have been turned into bed & breakfasts and several are open to the public and have museums attached. Many would make a good paddling destination, and I have included many of them in this guide.

Paddling Season: While some hardy souls paddle year-round (with the right equipment), March to early November are the best months. If you're looking for a wild ride, with high water in the rivers, try a late March or early April trip. That's when rivers' water flows are helped along by the winter runoff from snow and spring rains. Trips during April and May and again from September to early November can find rivers uncrowded. Watch out for the month of April, depending on the weather pattern—it can be cold, with temperatures in the 30s on some days.

State Forest Campgrounds: There are about 50 forest campgrounds, which are a good alternative to the often-crowded state parks. Many of these are on inland lakes and rivers. The campgrounds are rustic, with outhouses, water pumps, fire pits, and picnic tables.

State Parks: Paddlers should check out the state's nearly 60 state parks, most of which allow camping and are located on either the Great

Lakes, inland lakes, or rivers. The state parks are well used, have improved facilities (such as flush toilets and showers), and are equipped to handle recreational vehicles in need of power. Campsites can be reserved. Contact the state *Department of Natural Resources* (1-800-44-PARKS; www.michigan.gov/dnr). A state park sticker is required for entrance and there are camping fees.

Traffic and Highway Travel Tips: There's little traffic in much of rural Michigan, and you're generally doing the speed limit. The only exceptions are in the Detroit and Grand Rapids metro areas. There are no toll roads in Michigan. The only fee is $3.50 for crossing the Mackinac Bridge, which links the Upper and Lower peninsulas. The speed limits are 70 miles per hour on freeways, 65 on city expressways, and 55 on rural, two-lane roads. If coming from Canada, there can be backups at the Ambassador Bridge and the Detroit-Windsor Tunnel in Detroit, and the Blue Water Bridge in Port Huron.

Weather: The winters can be bone chilling and the summers hot and humid, with temperatures in the 90s. Because of the Great Lakes, winter hangs on longer in Michigan than in surrounding states, so springs tend to be short and often cold. During summer, cold fronts can blow in off the big lakes and temperatures can dip to 50 degrees and below. Paddlers should bring fleece and rain gear. A weather radio is handy.

Web Sites: The Pure Michigan tourism program has gained national attention for its advertising and promotion efforts. It maintains a travel site, www.michigan.org, which offers plenty of information about the state.

Welcome Centers: Michigan maintains 14 Welcome Centers throughout the state, and all offer good public facilities and plenty of information about paddling liveries, accommodations, restaurants, and attractions. The centers are staffed by people knowledgeable about their regions and who are willing to share information. If you're headed to the UP, make sure to stop at the St. Ignace Center, just past the toll booths; it has material for the entire UP. The other relevant centers and their locations are Ironwood, US 2; Menominee, US 41; Sault Saint Marie, I-75; Mackinaw City, I-75; Port Huron, I-94; and Monroe, I-75 northbound.

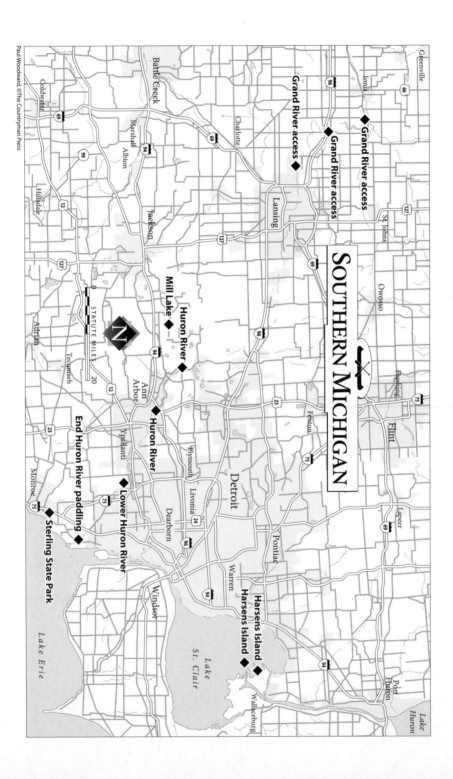

SOUTHERN MICHIGAN

Grand River access

Grand River access

Grand River access

Mill Lake

Huron River

Huron River

Huron River

End Huron River paddling

Lower Huron River

Sterling State Park

Harsens Island

Harsens Island

Detroit

Lansing

Jackson

Ann Arbor

Ypsilanti

Plymouth

Livonia

Dearborn

Warren

Pontiac

Fenton

Flint

Flushing

Laper

Port Huron

Owosso

St. Johns

Charlotte

Ionia

Greenville

Battle Creek

Marshall

Albion

Coldwater

Hillsdale

Adrian

Tecumseh

Monroe

Windsor

Wallaceburg

Lake St. Clair

Lake Erie

Lake Huron

N

STATUTE MILES
0   20

Paul Woodward, ©The Countryman Press

1 — Southern Michigan

Lake Erie, Huron River, Pinckney/Waterloo Recreation Areas, Lake St. Clair, Grand River

WITH MORE THAN 3 million people, this region is the most urbanized in the state—but that doesn't mean there isn't water to paddle. Lakes Erie and St. Clair are nearby, and paddlers have established a water trail on the Detroit River. There are also dozens of inland lakes, some of which have no motorboat traffic and little or no development. There's also the Huron River which winds around the metro Detroit area from Oakland County through Ann Arbor and eventually into Lake Erie.

Although paddling is done on Lake St. Clair, I'd stay away from it; it's crowded on weekends with motorboat and sailboat traffic. Try Lake Erie, there's less motorboat traffic.

A Few Compelling Reasons to Paddle in Southern Michigan

19 miles on the Huron River near Ann Arbor from Hudson Mills to Gallop Park, fast running water, three white-water rapids, the University of Michigan campus

Lake Erie sea kayaking at Sterling State Park, a big lake water challenge near Detroit

Mill Lake, Waterloo Recreation area, a lake without motorboats

1.   Lake Erie/Sterling State Park

Best Runs: Sterling State Park along Brest Bay, 12 miles, 8 hours
Accessibility: Good, with a boat launch at the state park
Skill Level: Beginner to intermediate
Best Times: May to Oct.
Description: Lake Erie is the shallowest of the Great Lakes, which
        means it can kick up quickly
Location: 5 miles north of Monroe off I-75

LAKE ERIE SHOULD BE the poster child for the environmental movement. In the 1960s it was called a "dead lake," with pollutants from Detroit's large population and industry along the Detroit River dumped in the waters and allowed to flow downriver and into the lake, killing fish and polluting beaches. These days anglers catch walleye and bathers lounge on its beaches.

The boat launch can be crowded during fishing season, but kayakers and canoeists can find spots at the edge of the concrete launch.

There are some fine freshwater marshes to paddle through before getting to the open lake, and there's also access to the Rasin River from the park. Look for ground-nesting birds; when I paddled the area in the early summer, I saw a mother swan and her young.

Most of the shoreline is in private hands, usually beach associations, so there's no place to stop for a picnic lunch—but it's doubtful there would be complaints about emergency landings.

Camping is available at the state park and there is a public bathing beach that could be used for swimming or to launch a watercraft.

2. Lake Erie Metro Park/
   Pointe Mouillee State Game Area

Best Runs: Paddle along costal wetland, with a trip up the Huron
        River
Accessibility: Good, with at boat launch in the park
Skill Level: Beginner to intermediate
Best Times: May to Oct.

Description: The Detroit and Huron rivers flow into Lake Erie
Location: Near South Rockwood, access via I-75

HERE'S A CHANCE to paddle along a 3-mile undeveloped coastline within a few miles of downtown Detroit—and add to that the coastal area of Pointe Mouillee, a wildfowl hunting area established in the 1870s, and there's a good day trip. The marshlands are prime bird-watching turf, and hawks and bald eagles are prime attractions. Nearby Sugar Island, Grosse Isle, and Celeron Island are within paddling distance, but watch for motorboat traffic.

It's a good place to watch lake freighters from a safe distance. The shipping channel is located well east of the park's waters.

The boat launch is located on the Huron River in the headquarters area. There are 4,000 acres and many lagoons and wetland areas to explore. This is not the place to be in September or October because it's heavily used by wildfowl hunters.

3. Huron River

Best Runs: Dexter/Ann Arbor area
Accessibility: Good, with access in numerous public parks
Skill Level: Beginner to intermediate
Best Times: Apr. to early Nov.
Description: The river is fairly slow moving and easy to paddle. Its course takes paddlers through several lakes (including Proud), which are good paddling destinations.
Fees: Entrance fees are required in the various public parks

THE RIVER RISES out of northern Oakland County and forms a semi-circle around much of metro Detroit, making it heavily used by paddlers and anglers—especially since access is good because of an extensive park system.

The river is mostly paddled in segments because of the 96 dams that must be gotten around. There have been efforts to remove the dams to allow for a free-flowing river, and at least one has been torn down. The dams range from large power facilities to just a few feet.

Enjoying a day on the river

However, the dams do produce lakelike impoundments for paddling, including Proud Lake, Kent Lake, and Island Lake—all of which are recreation areas with good public access.

Proud Lake Recreation Area to Kensington Metro Park (10 miles, 6 hours): Slow water, portages

The paddle starts in Proud Lake Recreation Area and takes you to Milford. Stay to the right in Proud Lake to follow the river channel. The first portage comes within about 2 miles and is around a dam to the right. The second comes in Milford—again, stay to the right. There's a take-out at Dawson Road Bridge, just below a canoe camp, and there are two boat launch areas in Kent Lake—the impoundment formed by the Kent Lake Dam, which is under I-96.

Kent Lake to Island Lake Recreation Area (10 miles, 6 hours): Lake paddling, a portage

There's a 5 mile paddle through Kent Lake and a portage around Kent Lake Dam under I-96, but then the Huron becomes a river again—although it's slow moving as it enters Island Lake Recreation Area and ranges from 30–40 feet wide and up to 3 feet deep. This section is undeveloped, and there's an opportunity for wildlife viewing. There's an access site 2 miles downstream of the dam, and then again 2 miles further at Riverbend Picnic Area. I'd suggest getting out of the river at Placeway Picnic Area in Island Lake and skipping the next few miles, as the river crosses under the busy US 23 freeway, and then for the next

12 miles there's no reasonable river access point. There is a take-out at Huron Meadows Metro Park near US 23, but it requires a nearly 800 foot portage. The river enters an area where it travels through extensive private property and four lakes. There's a state boat launch on Portage Lake, but it's mostly clogged with motorboat traffic, and I wouldn't suggest using it. The next viable put-in is at Hudson Hills Metro Park off Huron River Drive near Ann Arbor.

Hudson Mills to Gallop Park, Ann Arbor (19.5 miles, 12 hours): Whitewater and portages

This section is the best paddling on the river—with fast running water, three small white-water rapids to run, and decent public access at Hudson Mills Metro Park, Dexter-Huron Metro Park, Delhi Metro Park, and off W. Huron River Drive at Barton Pond.

The river ranges from 70–90 feet wide and is 1–3 feet in depth. Just before reaching Zeeb Road, paddlers encounter Rock Dam Rapids. There's a put-in off Zeeb Road just above it, with a foot trail. Basic skills are sufficient.

The river passes through private property until Delhi Metro Park. Here paddlers will encounter Delhi Rapids, which are more difficult;

A paddler gazes upon the undeveloped shore

some may want to portage. About 2.5 miles farther are Tubbs Rapids, which are easy.

The Huron slows as it enters a zone of private property and flows into Barton Pond, the backwaters of a power dam, which requires a portage to the right. For the next 2 miles the river slows as it moves toward Argo Dam, which must be portaged via the left channel. There's a serious effort to remove Argo. The river then moves gently through the city of Ann Arbor, where paddlers can see the University of Michigan campus, and the paddle ends at Island Park. Paddling pretty much ends in Ann Arbor. From there and for the next 12 miles, the river winds through the industrial areas of Ypsilanti, which include Ford and Belleville lakes and aren't worth paddling.

Lower Huron Metro Park to Lake Erie (17 miles, 8–9 hours): Extensive parkland, Lake Erie backwaters

River access is good from Lower Huron Metro Park off Hannan Road, south of Belleville and again at Willow Metro Park off Huron River Drive. The river is gentle and meanders its way toward Lake Erie where there is a take-out at Pointe Mouillee State Game Area, which is a paddling destination on Lake Erie (see Pointe Mouillee).

Outfitters

The Huron-Clinton Metro Parks (734-769-8686; www.metroparks .com). Canoe rentals are available at either Hudson Mills or Dexter and ending at Delhi Metro Park. The livery is open daily from early June to early September, and only on weekends during April and from September to October.

Skip's Huron River Canoe Livery (734-769-8686), Delhi Metro Park. Offers trips from Dexter-Huron Metro Park and Hudson Mills to Ann Arbor.

Gallop Park Canoe Livery (734-622-9319), 3000 Fuller Rd., Ann Arbor. Rents canoes and kayaks.

Heavner Canoe & Kayak (248-685-2379), 2775 Garden Rd., Milford. Offers boat rental and canoe/kayak car spotting on the upper Huron River.

4. Pinckney/Waterloo Recreation Areas

Best Runs: Trip through seven interconnected lakes starting in Bruin Lake
Accessibility: Good, with boat launches in two lakes
Skill Level: Beginner to intermediate
Best Times: Apr. to early Nov.
Description: Small, warm inland lakes
Location: West of Ann Arbor, access via I-94
Fees: Launching is free, entrance fees are required

THESE ARE MY local lakes, but I stay away from them on warm summer weekends—when they're clogged with recreational powerboaters, Jet Skiers, and anglers in powerful boats. Weekday evenings and the spring and fall are the best times to paddle the seven lakes with interconnected rivers and channels, as there are fewer powerboats.

There are boat launches at Bruin and Halfmoon lakes, and with a map you can navigate from lake to lake. Part of the fun is to find many of the hidden channels. In summer there's a good chance to spot rare sandhill cranes, which in Michigan only nest in this area and the eastern UP.

The recreation area offers camping (fees required), and nearby Chelsea has good restaurants and an art community—the centerpiece of which is the Purple Rose Theater (founded by actor Jeff Daniels, who still lives in the area).

Waterloo Recreation Area

Located nearly adjacent to Pinckney is the Waterloo Recreation Area, the home to one of my secret refuges—Mill Lake. It's small and only offers a few hours of paddling, but boat traffic is restricted to electric motors, so you'll only encounter a few anglers. It makes for a nice evening paddle.

Sandhill crane viewing is best done from a canoe

It's located just west of Chelsea and north off of I-94 at exit 156. The launch is off of McClure Road, not far from the Gerald Eddy Discovery Center. There are no fees.

Lake St. Clair/Detroit River

When Antonine de La Mothe Cadillac founded what was to become the city of Detroit in 1701, most of the 50 or so French Canadians he brought came by canoe, and Detroit—like many communities in the Great Lakes—started as a fur trading outpost. These days it's impossible to land a canoe or kayak on the Detroit River because over the last 300 years the entire riverfront has been walled by either concrete or steel, leaving little of the original shoreline.

The establishment of the Detroit Heritage River Water Trail is an attempt to bring a focus on paddling in the waterway, and some local kayakers paddle the river—but if you're a recreational paddler from out of state, it's not worth putting on your trip list. There are much better waters.

Most of the Lake St. Clair shoreline is highly developed, and although there are some boat marinas, they're busy with powerboats and sailboats during warm months; it's a chore to get on the water. One exception is Harsen's Island.

5. Lake St. Clair/Harsen's Island

Best Runs: Little and Big Muscamoot Bay
Accessibility: Difficult
Skill Level: Beginner to intermediate
Best Times: Apr. to Oct.
Description: Lake St. Clair marshlands
Home Base: Harsen's Island
Location: Southeast off I-94 via MI 29 to MI 154; ferry from mainland, a fee

ON HOT SUMMER WEEKENDS this is a party town for metro Detroiters with powerboats, and since it's less than an hour from the metro area's 3 million residents, it's a top destination. Again, if you're coming to

Michigan to paddle, don't put this spot on your list. It's mostly paddled by residents of the region looking for a quick trip. It's best during the week or early or late in the season.

The best access points to put you in Little and Big Muscamoot Bays are from the end of South Channel Drive, which is accessed from MI 154 and off Middle Channel Drive. Paddlers can explore the shoreline from either, and make trips to the historic Old South Channel Lighthouses and Gull Island. The St. Clair River channel can be explored, but there are lake freighters on it, along with lots of powerboat traffic.

6. Grand River

Best Runs: Grand Ledge to Portland
Accessibility: Fair
Skill Level: Beginner to intermediate
Best Times: Apr. to Oct.
Description: Slow moving, wide river, fairly shallow
Home Base: Grand Ledge/Portland

STRETCHING FROM NEAR Jackson to Grand Haven, the Grand is the state's longest river at 262 miles, and it offers some decent padding in its middle branch from Grand Ledge (near Lansing) to near Grand Rapids.

The entire length can be paddled, but I wouldn't suggest the trip for recreational paddlers. Access is limited, and there are too many meat grinder–like portages around an extensive system of power dams and low-head dams. This shouldn't be a destination for those coming from out of state, but because it runs through the populated southern Michigan region, it offers nearby paddling opportunities.

The best place to start is west of Lansing in the rural community of Grand Ledge, where there is a good put in place at a city park. Paddling opportunities are hampered by the lack of good access points.

Grand Ledge to Portage (27 miles, 8 hours): Rock formations,
a semiwild river

Put in at Jaycee Park off South River Street, and paddle past the 300-million-year-old sandstone ledges on the right that give the town its

Pausing to admire the ledges at Grand Ledge

name. Stay in the right channel to see them. There's a short portage to the left over a low-head dam, and after that it's clear sailing to Portland. There are a few homes along the river near Grand Ledge, but they give way to a semiwilderness area—especially in the Portland State Game Area, where the river winds around several islands. I saw otter, eagles, and wild turkey on one trip, though there are also black bear. The river is 40–50 feet wide and depths run from 1–3 feet, with some deeper holes. There are three emergency exits at county road bridges, but lifting a boat out at them would be difficult. Look for the charming old iron railroad bridges over the river; Portland itself also has two 19th century iron bridges. Take out at Thompson Field on Canal Street in Portland. There's a statue of legendary Michigan paddler Verlon Kruger at the field. Kruger organized epic river-length paddles of the Grand that take place every decade, the last in 2010.

Portland to Lyons (17 miles, 8 hours): Challenging portages, whitewater

If you're up for a challenge, this section takes paddlers through more undeveloped country, but at a price—two grueling portages of more than 100 yards each. Both portages are around functioning power dams, and there's an element of danger. The water forms two lakelike impoundments, which are slow paddling—especially on windy days. About 8 miles into the trip, the Grand becomes a river again, and there is one old collapsed dam that provides a minute or two of white-water fun. After that, it's a slow trudge into Lyons, a lovely little farm town, where there's another dam and difficult river exit. I'd end the trip here. The Grand continues to Grand Rapids, and eventually to Lake Michigan, but that part of the river takes paddlers through heavily used agricultural and urban areas.

In the Area

These bodies of water are in the Detroit metro area and near southern Michigan cities, which have many lodging and dining options.

Lodging

IN ANN ARBOR (HURON RIVER)

Vitosha Guest Haus (734-741-4969), 1917 Washtenaw Ave., Ann Arbor. This 10-room stone guesthouse is more of an inn than a B&B and would be a good place for a long stay. The rooms are large, all have private baths, and most have fireplaces. The stone building is an arts-and-crafts structure, and it is a relief from the Victorian frilliness that dominates many Michigan B&Bs. Rates $50–150.

Eating Out

IN ANN ARBOR (HURON RIVER)

Zingerman's Bakehouse (734-761-7255; www.zingermansbakehouse.com), 422 Detroit St., Ann Arbor. This place is just what the hungry paddler is looking for. It's an understatement to call it a deli—the sandwiches are all served on fresh Zingerman's bread. There are also many specialty food items. Prices $8–12.

    Casey's Tavern (734-665-6775), 304 Depot, Ann Arbor. Open daily for lunch and dinner. This is a popular neighborhood tavern with good burgers and a few weekly specials. It's near the Ann Arbor AMTRAK Station and is a good place to wait for the train. Prices $8–10.

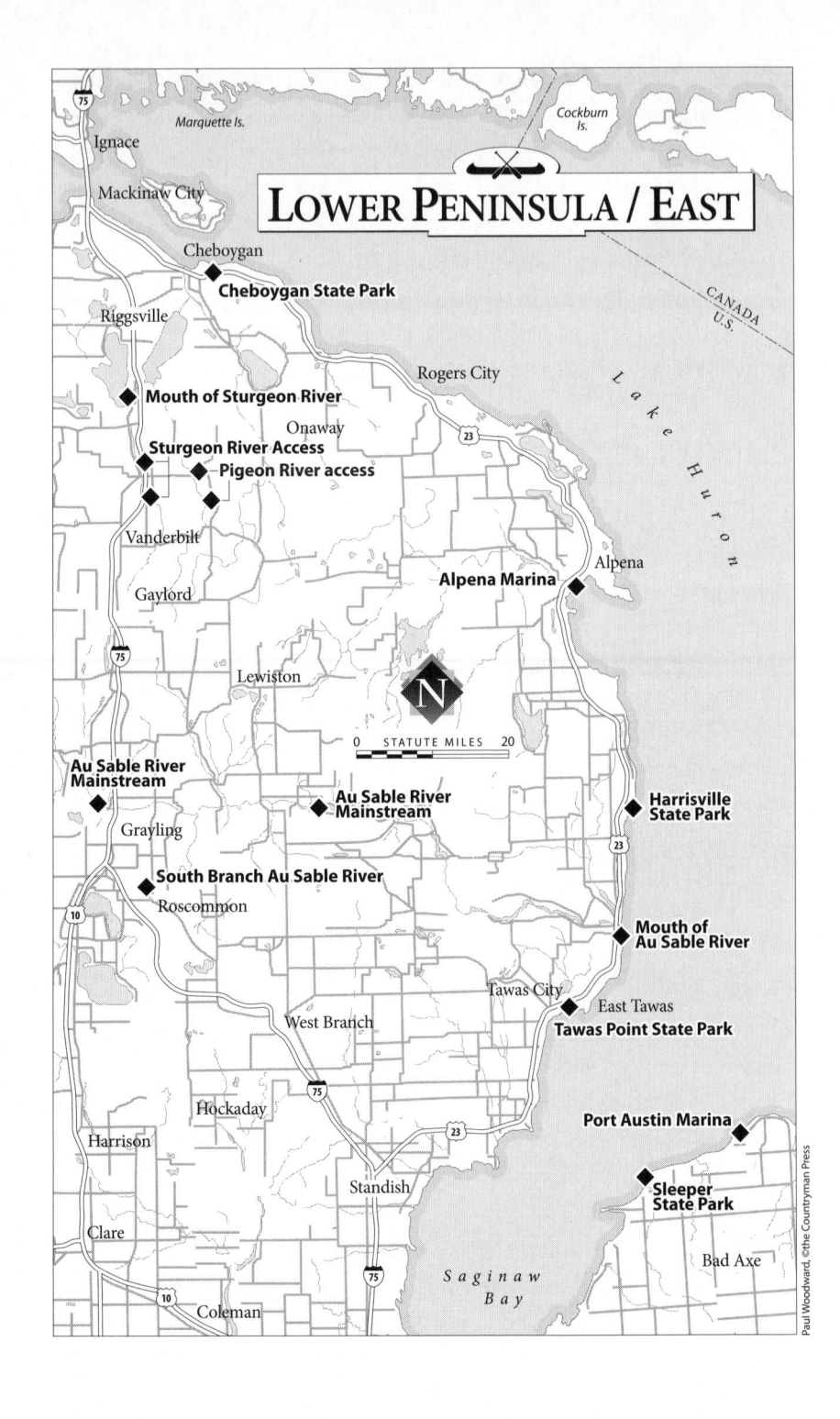

Marquette Is.

Cockburn Is.

Ignace

Mackinaw City

LOWER PENINSULA / EAST

CANADA
U.S.

Cheboygan

Cheboygan State Park

Riggsville

Rogers City

L a k e   H u r o n

Mouth of Sturgeon River

Onaway

Sturgeon River Access

Pigeon River access

23

Vanderbilt

Gaylord

Alpena Marina

Alpena

75

Lewiston

N

0   STATUTE MILES   20

Au Sable River Mainstream

Au Sable River Mainstream

Harrisville State Park

Grayling

South Branch Au Sable River

23

10

Roscommon

Mouth of Au Sable River

Tawas City

West Branch

East Tawas

Tawas Point State Park

Hockaday

75

23

Harrison

Port Austin Marina

Sleeper State Park

Standish

Clare

Bad Axe

S a g i n a w
B a y

75

10

Coleman

Paul Woodward, ©the Countryman Press

2 — Northeast Lower Peninsula

Au Sable River, Rifle River, Pigeon River, Sturgeon River; Lake Huron Area

THIS REGION IS a great destination, offering paddlers sea kayaking on Lake Huron, rivers to run, and flat water to paddle on inland lakes. While northwestern Michigan has been heavily developed and is a top tourist destination, the northeast has retained its backwoods feel and a traveler's dollar will go almost twice as far when it comes to lodging and eating out.

If You Had Five Days . . .

Day 1: Float the main stream of the Au Sable from Stephan Bridge to McMaster's Bridge. The six-hour trip takes paddlers past historic fly-fishing lodges and through pine woods. The river is fast, clear, and deep.

Day 2: If you're up for the challenge of fast water, make the run of the upper Sturgeon River near Wolverine. It's the fastest water in the Lower Peninsula and there are some tight turns.

Day 3: After two days in the woods, paddlers will welcome the open water of Tawas Bay in Lake Huron. Head to Tawas Point State Park and paddle the well-protected bay for the day.

Day 4: Head north to nearby Oscoda and the big waters of the Au Sable River near where it runs into Lake Huron.

Day 5: Head to Roscommon for a trip on the south branch of the Au Sable, but start at Chase Bridge Road and float through the semi-wild Mason Tract (which is undeveloped) to near the main stream.

The region's towns are low-key, homey places where most often the town tavern is the best option when it comes to eating out. They cater to the locals and sportspersons. Lodging is to be found mostly in mom-and-pop motels and rustic cabins. Camping is a good option.

But what it lacks in amenities, it makes up for in paddling possibilities. The storied Au Sable River system provides 120 miles of paddling from Grayling to Oscoda, and Rifle River near Rose City has nearly 50 miles of river. There are also three backwoods rivers—the Pigeon, Black, and Sturgeon—offering near-wilderness-style trips.

The Lake Huron coast, although offering less access than Lake Michigan, provides plenty of potential for sea kayaking—especially on protected Tawas Bay near Tawas City.

7. Au Sable River

Best Runs: Grayling to Oscoda, 120 miles, 4–6 days
Accessibility: Good
Skill Level: Beginner to intermediate
Best Times: Apr. to Oct.
Description: Clear, cold, fast running, spring-fed
Home Base: Grayling, Mio, and Oscoda

THE AU SABLE RIVER SYSTEM is a problematic padding destination. It's spring-fed and water levels don't dip in the summer, it's easily negotiated by beginner paddlers, much of it is in the Huron-Manistee National Forest, and there's good access. Because of those attractive reasons, it gets a lot of canoe/kayak and tubing traffic on summer weekends.

The river is also a major destination for fly anglers because of its consistent, predictable fly hatches—and miles of flies-only stretches of the river. Over the years there have been confrontations between anglers and paddlers, but if paddlers are courteous, there are few problems. I'm a paddler and an angler, and sometimes paddlers are so quiet, I can't hear them floating toward me.

Part of the problem is there are too many paddlers on the river on its main stream, just downstream from Grayling. The town is just off

If You Had Three Days . . .

Day 1: Put in at Stephan Bridge and float to McMaster's Bridge. This trip, which is realistically about six hours, takes you past the lovely, historic fly-fishing lodges on the river's main stream and through some less-developed riverbanks as you go along. There is one stretch upstream from McMaster's where you have to paddle—Conner's Flats, where the river broadens out and the flow slows. It speeds up near Rainbow Bend.

Day 2: Now it's time to see the big waters. Head to Mio and float to McKinley, a small riverside community with a tavern and gas station and store. The river broadens at Mio, and it's deeper. The water is big enough here to handle a lot of paddlers. If you have your own boat, an afternoon or evening trip would be good if you want to be alone.

Day 3: Float trip from Roscommon to Smith's Bridge, spending most of your time on the trip between Chase and Smith's Bridge in the Mason Tract, which is a nearly 3,000-acre wilderness area with no cabin development along the riverbanks. This section is rarely paddled by those on day trips. Much of the land in the tract was donated to the state by late George W. Mason, a Detroit industrialist.

If You Had Seven Days . . .

If you have the time and energy and want to camp along the way, take the 120-mile trip from Grayling to the mouth of the river at Oscoda.

Au Sable River History

The Au Sable River system drains nearly 2,000 square miles of northeastern Michigan, defines much of the region's history, and is still an important economic factor to the communities lying along its banks—which rely on tourism generated by paddlers and trout anglers.

The first paddlers in the region were Native Americans who crossed the state by canoe—using the Au Sable River system which drains into Lake Huron, and the Manistee River which connects to Lake Michigan. The two systems are near Grayling, and portages were made from one river to the other.

The first European paddlers were the French-Canadian fur trappers and traders in quest of beaver pelts that were eventually turned into hats for the well-to-do of Europe.

(continued)

Such activities had little impact on the river system—but then came the loggers who were after the virgin stands of white pine, which was sought after by builders because there were few knots in the wood and it could easily be sawed.

The loggers stacked the pine on the banks of the river during the winter cutting season and in the spring rolled them into the river and floated them to the mills. The logs caused much erosion to the sandy banks, and there are still log slides evident along the river—especially downriver from the Alcona Dam. The logs also scoured the river bottoms, destroying the vegetation and woody debris needed by fish to spawn.

The loggers were quickly followed by 19th-century sportsmen who were attracted by the grayling, a troutlike fish that's so easy to catch that the species quickly became extinct in the river—but not before lending its name to the town in Crawford County and turning the river into a 19th- and early-20th-century trout fishing destination. Trains ran regularly to the fishing towns, carrying anglers from Midwestern cities and beyond.

Many anglers eventually established lodges and fishing clubs on the banks of the Au Sable and nearby Manistee, many of which are 100 years old and can still be seen during paddling trips. Grayling is the hub for fishing and paddling. Trout Unlimited, the venerable fly-fishing organization, was founded there in 1959.

The paddling sports have a long tradition in the area, with canoe liveries the major draw to towns like Grayling, Mio, and Roscommon. The Au Sable River Canoe Marathon in late July attracts thousands of spectators to the banks of the river to watch the 120-mile race from Grayling to Oscoda. The first race was held in 1947.

The early loggers and anglers left another legacy, the Au Sable River boat. The flat-bottomed boats were first used by loggers to cart

I-75 and people arrive, rent a canoe/kayak or float tube, and get in the river there for a trip. That means that from late May to early September the river gets crowded from Grayling to Burtons Landing. With a little planning, you can avoid the crowds by paddling different sections of the river, even on weekends.

a floating cook shack along with them on river drives. The boats were very stable and could carry a lot of weight, but didn't need a lot of water to keep them floating.

They were adopted by fly anglers, and their building is now a cottage industry in the Au Sable River valley. There are no real plans for the boat and makers simply copy another boat, adding their own touches along the way. The boats are often 20 feet long, and are still made of wood. They are paddled and poled.

The sight of a varnished, wooden boat gently gliding along the river with a couple of anglers is a sight out of the 19th century. While many of the boats are individually owned and they can't be rented, there are fishing guides who will take a paddler out for a tour of the river for a fee. We've listed some of those guides in this book.

Anglers and an elegant Au Sable River boat

Have the outfitter drop you off at Burtons Landing and float to either Stephan or Wakeley bridges, both of which make for a good day trip. The best solution is to have your own boat. Canoe liveries usually want to be off the river at a certain time of day. With your own boat, you can set your own schedule, and be on the river during the early evening

A wooden canoe on the river

hours—which are often the nicest time of day.

As I've mentioned elsewhere in this guide, float times are a pet peeve. They're usually established by either the canoe livery or state or federal forest officials. Generally they're based on how long it takes for a canoe to float a river with the paddler doing nothing but steering.

Overestimating float times is a good way to do it; expect a four-hour float to take six hours, giving you plenty of time to enjoy the river.

My theory is to just about double the time on the river. If you fish, like I do, or just want to pause along the way for sight-seeing or hanging around a riverbank for nature viewing, you're going to burn up a lot of extra time. You're out there to enjoy yourself, not set a world paddling record. Plan on taking a shore lunch with you, and slow down. You're not on the clock.

Grayling to Wakeley Bridge (14 miles, 6–7 hours): Heavy canoe traffic

The paddle starts in downtown Grayling, but access is difficult, if you're paddling your own boat because most river property is in the hands of private canoe liveries. I use one of the liveries to spot my car downriver, where I want to get out, so I launch from their facility. There are better spots downriver to launch from, and you don't get caught up in the herd of paddlers who all seem to leave Grayling at the same time. The river is about 25 feet wide here and can get crowded as you pass by many river homes, and then under the I-75 freeway bridge. It's here that the paddling really starts, the river widens to 50 feet and more, and there are fewer homes. Watch for fly anglers in the river. There are plenty of hardwoods, making it a good fall foliage paddle. You'll pass by Burton's Landing, Keystone Landing, and a canoe campground. All can be used for camping.

Wakeley Bridge to Parmalee Bridge (16.5 miles, 5–6 hours): Less traffic, slow water

The river slows here and there's less canoe traffic. Paddlers will need to pick up their pace, but the real slowdown comes shortly after passing Whitepine Canoe Forest Campground when the south branch feeds in. This stretch of the river is called Conner's Flats and it lives up to its name as the water widens out and slows down. There are take-outs at Rainbow Bend Campground, which isn't well marked, and at McMaster's Bridge. The water speeds up again after the north branch feeds into the main stream, and there are some rocks to dodge.

Parmalee Bridge to Mio Dam (12.5 miles, 4–6 hours): Faster water, portage around dam

This is one of my favorite floats for fly-fishing; it usually takes me eight or nine hours, because I'm fishing along the way. But even if you don't fish, it's a good section to take your time on—the river is fast, clean, and cool, and there are riffles. There's little riverbank development, and good wildlife viewing. Camping is available at Luzerne Free Park a short distance from Parmalee Bridge and there's river access at Camp 10 Bridge, at the beginning of Mio Pond. There are state forest campgrounds and access on the northern and southern sides of the pond. The dam portage is to the right, and isn't difficult.

Mio Dam to McKinley Bridge (14.5 miles, 5–6 hours): Paddling the big waters

The river widens to nearly 100 feet below the dam and it's often floated by drift boats piloted by fishing guides pursuing the large trout in the river here. There are occasional encounters between paddlers and drift boats, so simply paddle around them; the river is big enough to accommodate a lot of traffic. The river passes through the Huron-

An Au Sable bridge crossing

Manistee National Forest, which allows camping on the shoreline. Look for an established campsite; it's a well-used area and there are plenty. The take-out is at McKinley, a charming little trout fishing village with cabins along the riverbank.

McKinley Bridge to Alcona Dam (11 miles, 4–5 hours): More big water, a portage

More big water here, with little road access, but an undeveloped shoreline gives you a wild feeling. I linger here when I paddle this section. You may want to take out at FR 4001—not only to avoid a portage, but also the heavy powerboat and Jet Ski traffic on the impoundment. Several private and public campgrounds attract boaters. The portage around the dam is on the right.

Alcona Dam to Five Channels Dam (18 miles, 5–7 hours): Dam discharge, difficult portage

Recreational paddlers may want to skip this section of the river because quick releases of water from the dam raise the river level several feet without much warning. I was fishing this section when it happened and it came as a shock. There's plenty of National Forest Service land to camp on. There's also a 250-yard portage to the right and a shorter, but steep, one to the left.

Five Channels Dam to Foote Dam (15 miles, 6–9 hours): Impoundment paddling, portages

Paddling can be difficult through this impoundment of the upcoming dam, Cooke. The banks are high and it's a delight to view the undeveloped shoreline. There are plenty of campsites. The Cooke Dam portage is to the left and isn't difficult.

Foote Dam to Oscoda (11.5 miles, 3–4 hours): Deep waters, anglers in spring/fall

Paddlers may want to skip this section in the spring and fall when the annual steelhead and salmon runs are on. The wide, deep river is fairly slow and it meanders through hardwoods to the mouth of the river in Oscoda. There's a public boat launch for a take-out.

Outfitters

IN GRAYLING

Penrods (888-467-4837; www.penrodscanoe.com), 100 Maple St., Grayling. Canoe/kayak trips on the upper portions of the Au Sable. Vehicle spotting services.

Borchers (989-348-4921; www.canoeborchers.com), 101 Maple St., Grayling. Canoe/kayak rentals for day and multiday trips as far as the river mouth in Oscoda. Vehicle spotting services.

Carlisle Canoes (989-348-2301; www.carlislecanoes.com), 110 State St., Grayling. Rentals and trips through the river to Oscoda. Vehicle spotting services.

IN MIO

Gotts' Landing (989-826-3411; www.gottslanding.com), off MI 33 at the Au Sable River, Mio. Canoe/kayak rentals, trips from Mio to Lake Huron.

Hinchman Canoe Livery (989-826-3267; www.hinchman.com), off MI 33 at the Au Sable River, Mio. Trips as far as Lake Huron, rentals of canoes/kayaks.

8.   Au Sable River, South Branch

Best Runs: Roscommon to the Au Sable main stream
Accessibility: Good
Skill Level: Beginner to intermediate
Best Times: Apr. to Oct.
Description: Fast running, clear water
Home Base: Roscommon

MOST FOLKS PADDLE only the upper portion of the Au Sable's south branch (from Roscommon to Chase River Bridge) and miss the best part of the river—from Chase Bridge to the Au Sable's main stream. That's because most of the canoe liveries are located in Roscommon.

Because of that, paddlers miss the experience of traveling through the Mason Tract, a 5,300-acre wild area given to the state by auto executive George Mason. His intent was to keep the area in a wild state, a good insight for an industrialist who made his money on manufacturing in the Detroit area during an era that wasn't known for being conservation-minded.

The Mason Tract is a favored spot for fly anglers seeking solitude, so they aren't wild about paddlers. But I both fly-fish and paddle, and hope to show you a way to paddle the river without disturbing the anglers.

The trip is well worth it—there are bear, deer, herons, and other wildlife to see. The river is fairly wide and deep, so that it's easily paddled; but it's also a fairly short trip, so why not just drift it? There's no rush. Apart from wildlife and great scenery, there are also historical sites—Durant's Castle and the Mason Chapel. There are signs and they're worth getting out of the river to see.

The castle was built by an early founder of General Motors, Billy Durant, who developed the parcel where the castle sits. There was once a large stone home on the site, but it has since burned.

The paddle from Chase Bridge Road to the main stream is only a couple of hours. If you're looking for a full day, try the paddle from Roscommon to the main stream. The upper portion of the river is lined with cottages and homes, so I'd suggest making short work of that portion of the river—use your time on the Chase Bridge to the main stream portion.

Steckert Road to Chase Bridge (3 miles, 2–3 hours): Restricted access, heavy traffic

I had the worst paddling experience of my life on this section due to heavy canoe traffic on a fall weekend. Not only were there too many canoes on this small, 30- to 75-foot-wide river, but the paddlers' behavior was crude. Enough said. There's lots of riverside development, so if you're looking for a quality experience, skip this section and head down river to Chase Bridge, where the Mason Tract starts.

Chase Bridge to Smith Bridge (10 miles, 4–6 hours): Better waters, a place to linger

This is the best place to put in to avoid the hoards of paddlers. Access is good at a bridge off Chase Bridge Road, and the paddle takes you through the undeveloped Mason Tract where you can experience semi-wilderness paddling. There's a two-tract road that follows the river, but it's mostly used by anglers who use footpaths for river access. The Canoe Harbor state campground just upstream from Smith Bridge offers 45 sites, with rustic facilities.

Smith Bridge to Conner's Flats (7.5 miles, 3–4 hours): River widens, deep holes

The river gets up to 85 feet wide and 5 feet deep as it slowly works its way to the main stream. Cottages dot the banks. The next access points are on the main stream at Conner's Flats Public Access and Rainbow Bend (see Au Sable River).

Outfitters

Paddle Brave Canoe Livery & Campground (989-275-5273, www .paddlebrave.com), 10610 Steckert Bridge Rd., Roscommon. Canoe/ kayak and tube rental for trips on the south branch, with shuttle service. The campground has 33 sites with electricity.

    Hiawatha Canoe Livery (989-275-5213; www.canoehiawatha

Many canoe/kayak liveries dot Michigan shores

.com), 1113 Lake St., Roscommon. Canoe/kayak trips to Steckert Bridge, Chase Bridge, and from Chase to Smith Bridge. Shuttle service is provided.

9. Rifle River

Best Runs: The 47 miles from the Rifle River Recreation Area near Lupton to near Omer

Accessibility: Good. There are eight access points: Sage Lake Road, Teters Road, Ladds Landing, Greenwood Road Bridge, Maple Ridge Road, Melita Road, River Road, and Stover Road.

Skill Level: Beginner to intermediate.

Best Times: May to Oct.

Description: Narrow, fast in spots, few obstacles

Home Base: Rose City, Lupton

Location: Southern portion, northeast Lower Peninsula, off MI 33

BECAUSE IT'S ONE of the closest Up North rivers to southern Michigan cities, it is paddled by the party crowd whose idea of a fun float trip is to lash several canoes together for use as a party barge. You'd wish these folks would simply rent a pontoon boat on a lake and have at it. There has been a lot of bad behavior on this river, including a controversial case when a sheriff's deputy ticketed a paddler for using obscene language, and the canoeist fought it in court, citing his First Amendment rights.

If you're into the party scene, have at it—but for others I wouldn't recommend floating the river during summer weekends. Try earlier in the season or during weekdays. If you're in the area and want better paddles, try the south branch of the Au Sable, Pigeon, Black, or Sturgeon rivers for better wilderness experiences. All are included in this guide.

That said, the river is lovely, winding its way through pines and hardwoods to its destination on Saginaw Bay. This would make a good fall paddle to see the foliage.

Twin Lake Road to Maple Ridge Road Bridge (22 miles, 9–10 hours): Low water in summer

The river can be paddled from the Rifle River Recreation Area north of Sage Lake Road (or from that road), but paddlers will have a better experience if they put in at Twin Lake—where there's a state forest campground with good river access. The water above that point is too shallow, especially during the summer. Ballad Bridge, just below the campground, is also a good option. The water quickens and deepens as you go, but look for boulders and large rocks that can flip you over. Much of the riverbank is private property. Paddling traffic picks up at Selkirk Bridge, where a canoe livery operates, and the water widens to 30–50 feet. Below MI 55 there are rapids—during warmer months expect to get out of the boat and pull it over them.

Moffatt Bridge to Old MI 70 (10 miles, 3.5–5 hours): A good kid's paddle

The river runs up to 100 feet wide here and there are some rocks to dodge, but generally it's an easy family paddle. When the river is low in summer, follow the deeper channels. There's a good take-out place with parking at Old MI 70. The river continues another 10 miles through the city of Omer, with the last take-out at Stover Road. From there the river goes into Saginaw Bay.

Outfitters

White's Canoe Livery (989-654-2654; www.whitescanoe.com), Sterling. Offers rentals and owns several campgrounds along the river.

   River View Campground & Canoe Livery (989-654-2447; www.riverviewcampground.com), 5755 N. Townline Rd., Sterling. Canoes, tubes, and kayaks for rent, along with campgrounds and cabins.

   Rifle River Campground & Canoe Livery (989-654-2556; www.riflerivercampground.com), 5825 Townline Rd., Sterling. Canoe/kayak rentals, plus tubes. The campground has more than 80 sites.

10. Pigeon River

Best Runs: Red Bridge to Mullett Lake, 17 miles
Accessibility: Fair
Skill Level: Intermediate to advanced
Best Times: May to Oct.
Description: An easily paddled wilderness river
Home Base: Vanderbilt, Wolverine, Gaylord
Location: North central Lower Peninsula, off I-75 north of
   Gaylord
Boat Suggestion: Small river kayaks rather than a canoe

THIS RIVER AND I are old friends—I've fished it, cross-country skied near it, and paddled it for more than 30 years, and I find myself going back to it again and again. The paddling is nothing special and fairly easy, but it's the 98,000-acre Pigeon River Country State Forest that keeps me coming back.

   It's the home of the state's elk, the only one east of the Mississippi. There are special viewing areas in the state forest for the public. There are also black bear, deer, grouse, and other birds worth watching.

   There's little development on the Pigeon, so it's my alternative to the Au Sable River, 30 minutes to the south, in the summer—when it gets too crowded. I've fished the section between Sturgeon Valley Road and Webb Road many times in the summer, and rarely see paddlers. The river there can be too shallow during the summer.

Sometimes, unfortunately, woody debris likes the river channel as much as you do

There are no canoe liveries on the river (only one in nearby Wolverine), so paddlers will need to bring their own boats.

Red Bridge to Mullet Lake (17 miles, 5–6 hours): Tight turns, fallen trees

There's a price to pay for leaving the crowds behind—some tough paddling. Make sure your maneuvering skills are in place before tackling this stretch. The river is 30–40 feet wide and up to 3 feet deep, but it's fairly slow. The next take-out place is Afton Road, about 6 miles downriver. Near Pigeon River Road, the river widens up to 60 feet and the current picks up. Just after the MI 68 Bridge, the river becomes challenging. Beginners may want to take out at MI 68, there's good parking and access. There's rapids below the bridge and trees across the river, requiring paddlers to either lift their boat over the obstruction while in the river or portage. As the river nears Mullett Lake, it slows. The take-out is at Mullett Lake Road.

Outfitters

Henley's Canoe & Kayak (231-525-9994; www.henleysrentals.com), Wolverine City Park. Jon Henley holds forth here in a restored train depot with rental canoes, kayaks, and tubes for float trips—and good river information. He'll also handle vehicle spotting for those using their own boats.

11. Sturgeon River

Best Runs: Towbridge Road to Burt Lake, 16 miles, 8 hours
Accessibility: Good
Skill Level: Beginner to intermediate
Best Times: May to Oct.
Description: Fast running, 13.8 feet per mile
Home Base: Wolverine
Location: North central Lower Peninsula, off I-75 north of Gaylord

IT'S ONE OF the fastest-flowing rivers in the Lower Peninsula, and for experienced paddlers it's a good skills test, but one not to be taken lightly by novices. The river flows mostly through public lands, so there's a semiwilderness feel to it, but at times that feel is broken by the sounds of traffic coming from I-75—which runs parallel to the river.

Most paddling is done from Wolverine, where there's a good public access site at Wolverine City Park and a canoe livery nearby. A standard 17-foot canoe would work well, but a small river kayak would be easy to maneuver and fun on the rapids. There's also a bike trail running through town for folks looking for a bike/paddling vacation.

There's not much to find in the way of accommodations or restaurants in Wolverine, but the Indian River area (about 10 miles north) is a large resort community, and better services can be found. Gaylord is about 17 miles to the south, and is a major tourist town with chain hotels/motels and restaurants.

Towbridge Road to Burt Lake (16 miles, 8 hours): Fast waters,
Class I–II rapids

There's an access point off Towbridge Road near I-75, but you're going to need some help from Jon Henley at his canoe livery in Wolverine to find it. He's an affable guy and helpful. The upper river is narrow, 15–30 feet, and can be shallow in July and August—but it can be an enjoyable ride. Watch for tight turns and logs across the river. Things change at Wolverine Park, where the river widens to 30–50 feet and slows. It also deepens as you head toward Haakwood State Forest Campground, another good access point; it's near a railroad bridge. Just past the campground near White Road Bridge there are some Class I–II rapids that can usually be run, even during the dryer summer months. Fisher Woods Road is the best take-out spot, with good access and parking. Shortly after that the river enters Burt Lake, and just to the west is Burt Lake State Park, a good take out point. Camping is available.

Outfitters

Henley's Canoe & Kayak (231-525-9994; www.henleysrentals.com), Wolverine City Park. Jon Henley holds forth here in a restored train depot with rental canoes, kayaks, and tubes for float trips—and good river information. He'll also handle vehicle spotting for those using their own boats.

Lake Huron Area

Saginaw Bay, Tawas Bay, Harrisville, Alpena, Cheboygan/Bois Blanc Island, Mackinac Island

THE LAKE HURON SHORELINE has always been the poor sister to Lake Michigan because it doesn't have the wide, sandy beaches (and public access can be difficult), but sea kayakers should not cross it off their paddling list.

The prevailing westerly winds helped create those sandy beaches, but also produce some pretty hefty waves along the shoreline. Lake Huron is in the lee of those winds, and the lake isn't as rough—just what kayakers are looking for. State parks and public beaches provide the best water access on the Huron coast, locally known as the sunrise side.

A kayaker prepares to launch into Lake Huron

Saginaw Bay has a tremendous potential to be a kayaking destination—with its shallow, warm waters and gentle shoreline—but it's an agricultural region and there's a lack of public access. The southeast side of Saginaw Bay is called the Thumb by Michigan residents who often show people where they live by holding up their hand and pointing to a certain spot.

For some reason, most folks

If You Had Five Days . . .

Day 1: A day trip out of Port Austin to see the sandstone cliffs at Pointe aux Barques and the Port Austin Reef Light.

Day 2: A day trip around Tawas Point, a sandy spit of land in Lake Huron, which has a lighthouse.

Day 3: A stop at Harrisville State Park for a trip around Harrisville Harbor.

Day 4: A paddle along Huron Beach.

Day 5: An overnight stay on Mackinac Island and a day tour of its coastland.

from southern Michigan get on the freeway system and head north for recreation, bypassing the Thumb region. Sea kayakers should give this region more consideration, especially as a weekend destination. The Caseville area, Pointe aux Barques, and Grindstone City all have shorelines worth seeing.

Saginaw Bay and Lake Huron shoreline communities have a genuine small town feel to them because they've avoided the gentrification that's occurred along Lake Michigan. Lodging and restaurants are usually of the mom-and-pop variety, but come at low prices.

Sea kayakers could spend a week exploring the Lake Huron coast, without seeing too many other folks on the water.

12. Saginaw Bay

Best Runs: A paddle off Pointe aux Barques
Accessibility: Fair
Skill Level: Beginner to intermediate
Best Times: May to Oct.
Description: Saginaw Bay is shallow and can be mucky
Home Base: Caseville, Port Austin

Caseville

The park is off MI 25 northeast of Caseville; although it doesn't have a formal boat launch, it's an easy boat carry from the parking lot to Saginaw Bay. While much of the bay has a fairly muddy shoreline, the Caseville area has sandy beaches and the water is fairly shallow. There are two county parks that could be paddled to—Hat Point to the east and another several miles to the west; otherwise, most of the shoreline is in private hands.

Albert E. Sleeper State Park (989-856-4411; www.dnr.state.mi.us /parksandtrails) 6573 State Park Rd., Caseville. The park offers a swimming beach and facilities, along with camping in cabins or on campsites. There is a fee.

Pointe aux Barques

Located at the tip of the Thumb, this area offers kayakers views of lighthouses, sandstone cliffs, and the remnants of a once-thriving industry—grindstone making at Grindstone City. However, there are only three access points, making it difficult for paddlers to get on the water.

My favorite spot is Grindstone City, where there's a public boat launch off MI 25. Nearby are old, 19th-century round grindstones that were once manufactured here and shipped around the Midwest to mills which used them to grind grain into flour. A good day trip would be to the east to see the Pointe aux Barques Lighthouse, which dates from 1847 and is now a museum open to the public. There's a small, informal boat launch near the lighthouse. It's about a 10 mile round-trip from Grindstone City to the lighthouse.

There's another launch site in Port Austin at a public marina in the downtown area just off MI 25, and from there it's an easy paddle to the west to see the sandstone cliffs and several sea caves—uncommon in this area. There's also the Port Austin Reef Lighthouse, which was built in 1878 to alert mariners about the shallow waters. The area receives a lot of attention from anglers, so expect some competition for boat launching space. The other access point is Port Crescent State Park, about 3 miles west of Port Austin.

Port Crescent State Park (989-738-8663; www.dnr.state.mi.us /parksandtrails), 1775 Port Austin Rd. The park has a 3-mile sandy beach from which paddlers can launch. There are campsites and a small cabin for rent. There is a fee.

13. Tawas Bay

Best Runs: A paddle off Tawas Point
Accessibility: Good from Tawas Point State Park
Skill Level: Beginner to intermediate
Best Times: May to Oct.
Description: Tawas Bay is protected from the open lake by the point
Home Base: Tawas City/East Tawas

TAWAS POINT IS sometimes called the Cape Cod of the Midwest, and while that's a bit of a chamber of commerce exaggeration, it's a pleasant, sandy point on Lake Huron, which can often be stony.

Anglers and sailors are attracted to the bay and there can be some boat traffic, but the sailboats stick to deeper water and the fishing boats are generally small.

The state park offers camping and the restored Tawas Lighthouse in the park is worth a stop. Although there's no formal boat launch, a canoe or kayak could be easily put in the water at the swimming beach near the campground.

The trip around Tawas Bay is about 10 miles, and would make a

Lake Huron from a kayak's-eye view

good day trip. A good lunch stop would be at the Tawas City Park beach. From there, paddlers could even walk to the downtown area.

14. Harrisville

Best Runs: A paddle from the state park
Accessibility: Good from Harrisville State Park
Skill Level: Beginner to intermediate
Best Times: May to Oct.
Description: Open waters of Lake Huron
Home Base: Harrisville

THE CITY IS a genuine small American town of about 500 residents, and is perched on Harrisville Harbor on Lake Huron. Unlike many Lake Michigan towns, Lake Huron communities have escaped gentrification, giving them a genuine small town feel. A paddling trip from Harrisville State Park will give you a view of the downtown.

Resources

Harrisville State Park (989-724-5126; www.dnr.state.mi.us/parks andtrails), 248 State Park Rd., Harrisville. There's no formal launching spot, but it's a short carry to the shoreline from the parking lot. Camping is available. Fees are charged.

15. Alpena

Best Runs: A paddle in protected Thunder Bay
Accessibility: Fair
Skill Level: Beginner to intermediate
Best Times: May to Oct.
Description: Open waters of Lake Huron
Home Base: Alpena

THERE ARE ABOUT two hundred shipwrecks in Lake Huron's Thunder Bay off the coast of Alpena that can be best seen from a kayak tour. They're in the Thunder Bay National Marine Sanctuary, created to protect the mostly 19th-century ships from being plundered by divers. Access to the bay is from the Alpena Marina—but before going it alone, stop at the Great Lakes Maritime Heritage Center and consider going on a tour with an outfitter, which will better help paddlers locate the wrecks.

Outfitters

Green Planet Extreme (517-242-4752; www.greenplanetextreme.com). This outfitter operates from various locations in the state and offers shipwreck tours from Alpena.

Resources

Thunder Bay National Marine Sanctuary (989-356-8805; www.thunder bay.noaa.gov), 500 W. Fletcher St., Alpena. There are displays and information at the Great Lakes Maritime Heritage Center, where the sanctuary is located. Divers can view the wrecks, but nothing can be brought up. There are glass-bottom boat and kayak tours of the ships, and seven lighthouses in the area that can also be toured. The center is a good place to start.

16. Cheboygan/Bois Blanc Island

> **Best Runs:** A paddle in protected Duncan Bay
> **Accessibility:** Fair
> **Skill Level:** Beginner to intermediate
> **Best Times:** May to Oct.
> **Description:** Open waters of Lake Huron
> **Home Base:** Cheboygan

DOWNTOWN CHEBOYGAN IS a bit of an industrial town, but just east of it is Cheboygan State Park, which provides good access from its parking areas for paddlers who want to explore the shallow and protected Duncan Bay. For the adventurous there's a passenger ferry to 34-square-mile Bois Blanc Island, much of it in the Mackinaw State Forest, which provides lake access to paddlers.

Access

Plaunt Transportation (231-627-2354; www.bbiferry.com), 412 Water St., Cheboygan. Operates daily from May to November, reservations are suggested. Round trip for a car or small truck is $50.

Resources

Cheboygan State Park (231-627-2811; www.michigandnr.com /parksandtrails), 4490 Beach Rd, Cheboygan. There's a boat launch and camping available. Fees charged.

17. Mackinac Island

> **Best Runs:** A paddle around the island
> **Accessibility:** Fair
> **Skill Level:** Beginner to intermediate
> **Best Times:** May to Oct.
> **Description:** Open waters of Lake Huron
> **Home Base:** Mackinac Island

THE HISTORIC ISLAND in the Straits of Mackinac is a top travel destination in Michigan, known for having no vehicles and offering horse carriage rides and bicycling around the island. The Victorian era is still alive at the Grand Hotel, the island's centerpiece, which has the longest wooden porch in the country. Increasingly, kayakers are paying attention to the island—but it's a problematic destination in that transporting boats to the island can be difficult, and its waters can be tricky at times. If you want to paddle the island, I'd suggest going on a group tour with a guide.

Outfitters

Woods & Water Ecotours (906-484-4157; www.woodswaterecotours .com), 20 Pickford Rd., Hessel. Owner Jessie Hadley has a gem of an enterprise here, offering kayak lessons, tours, and extended trips to the islands—nearby Drummond Island, Isle Royale in Lake Superior, and Mackinac Island. There are also all-woman tours offered. Rates range from $65 for a two-hour lesson to $125 for a full day of paddling. Extended trips range from $550–750.

    Green Planet Extreme (517-242-4752; www.greenplanetextreme .com). This outfitter operates from various locations in the state and offers shipwreck tours from Alpena.

In the Area

Lodging

IN GRAYLING (AU SABLE RIVER)

Rayburn Lodge B&B (989-348-7482; www.rayburnlodgebnb.com), 1491 Richardson Rd., Grayling. After a day on the river, why not spend the night next to it? This 1930s lodge is a good example of those built in the early 20th century by well-to-do fly anglers, and it's just what you would expect—a rustic log cabin with a massive fieldstone fireplace. Anglers can step outside and wet a line in what anglers consider the "Holy Waters" section of the Au Sable. Reservations are required. Rates from $95–125.

Borchers Canoe and Kayak (989-348-4921; www.canoeborchers .com), 101 Maple St., Grayling. Mark and Cheri Hunter run a top-notch operation, offering both lodging in a bed & breakfast–style inn and canoe and kayak rental. The six rooms are located next to the river, and you can pop into your boat for a day on the river after a fine breakfast served by Cheri. There's a delightful second-story porch with a view of the river. There are also room and canoe rental packages. Rates from $75–100.

Penrod's (989-348-2912; www.penrodscanoe.com), 100 Maple St., Grayling. There are 14 cozy log cabins, some with cooking facilities, located on a 7-acre site along the Au Sable River. The interiors evoke a rustic feeling and have knotty-pine paneling and pine beds and furnishings. The cabins are great for larger groups and families, with some accommodating up to four or more persons. Penrod's also offers canoes and kayaks for rent, and also shuttle service (and spotting services for those with their own boats). Rates from $60–100.

IN MIO (AU SABLE RIVER)

Au Sable Valley Inn (989-826-1737; www.ausablevalleyinn.com), 515 Lockwood Ln., Mio. A newer place with simple but clean motel rooms. Rates from $70–80.

Hinchman Acres Resort (989-826-3267; www.hinchman.com), off MI 33 at the Au Sable River, Mio. Open May through October. The resort has 11 cottages on 17 acres along the river, all with fully equipped kitchens. Rates from $50–150.

NEAR ROSCOMMON (AU SABLE RIVER, SOUTH BRANCH)

Better lodging is in the Houghton/Higgins Lakes area 5–10 miles from Roscommon

Spring Brook Inn (1-800-424-0218; www.springbrookinn.com), 565 W. West Branch Rd. (MI 55), Houghton Lake. The inn offers eight upscale rooms, some with hot tubs and fireplaces, and a casual dining restaurant. Rates from $65–125.

IN TAWAS CITY (LAKE HURON)

Days Inn Tawas City (989-362-0088; www.daysinntawas.com), US 23, downtown Tawas City on the bay. This 42-room hotel offers large modern rooms, some with hot tubs. There's an indoor pool, and a restaurant on the premises. Rates from $75–100.

NEAR WOLVERINE (STURGEON RIVER, PIGEON RIVER)

Brentwood Lodging (231-238-7310; www.brentwoodlodging.com), 4778 S. Straits Hwy., Indian River. They have houses, cabins, and motel rooms, some with efficiency kitchens. Rates from $55–120.

Star Gate Motel (231-238-7371; www.stargatemotel.com), 4646 S. Straits Hwy., Indian River. Basic, but clean, traditional style motel with one- and two-bedroom units. Rates from $50–76.

Eating Out

IN GRAYLING (AU SABLE RIVER, MANISTEE RIVER)

Spike's Keg 'O' Nails (989-348-7113), 301 James St., Grayling. This is a longtime favorite of travelers and locals alike, and offers classic pub food in a family-style tavern. It's the kind of place that goes an extra mile for their customers. Several years ago I stumbled in there with my two hungry sons during a fishing trip. A storm had hit the area, and the power was out. The staff set up candles on the tables and bar, and were serving hungry people whatever they could scrounge up. Because of that, I always stop there. Prices from $5–15.

Westside Diner (989-344-0710), 6301 W. MI 72, Grayling. This small place is high on the list of places to eat for locals, with its focus on traditional homemade diner food. Prices from $6–15.

IN MIO (AU SABLE)

Au Sable River Restaurant (989-826-3590), on MI 33, Mio. This is just the place for paddlers—with decent-sized meals; breakfast, lunch, and dinner; and daily specials. It's a clean, large place and is frequented by local residents. Prices from $8–12.

NEAR ROSCOMMON (SOUTH BRANCH, AU SABLE RIVER)

East Bay Grille Restaurant (989-366-6347; www.springbrookinn.com), 565 W. West Branch Rd. (MI 55), Houghton Lake. This upscale grill is a real find in this area, with a menu that includes prime rib, steak, lamb, chicken, pork, seafood, fish, and pasta. There's a bar. Prices from $18–26.

IN GAYLORD (STURGEON RIVER, PIGEON RIVER)

The Sugar Bowl (989-732-5524), 216 W. Main, Gaylord. Open for lunch and dinner. The family-owned restaurant has been a favorite of locals since 1919 and keeps people coming back for its traditional American menu of steaks, seafood, and pub fare. Prices from $10–20.

Bennethum's Northern Inn (989-732-9288), 3917 Old 27 South, Gaylord. Open daily for lunch and dinner. There is a decent wine list for this area, and the food offerings range from fish and chips to seafood, pasta, and steaks. The place has a North Woods ambiance. Entrees from $15–25.

Timothy's Pub (989-732-9333), 110 S. Otsego Ave., Gaylord. This is where the locals gather for the traditional Friday fish fry and burgers. Prices from $8–10.

IN TAWAS CITY (LAKE HURON)

Mulligan's Irish Pub (989-362-8482), 214 Newman St., Tawas City. This is a local's hangout that offers pub food in a casual tavern setting. Prices from $8–12.

NEAR WOLVERINE (STURGEON RIVER)

The Brown Trout Restaurant & Tavern (231-238-9441; www.thebrown trout.com), 4653 S. Straits Hwy., Indian River. Diners aren't going to find a better menu to choose from in the region. The full service restaurant offers lunch and dinner, and has a special smoked trout chowder. They feature steak, pork, seafood, chicken, pasta, and pizza in a casual, historic atmosphere. The place dates back to the 1930s. Prices from $10–25.

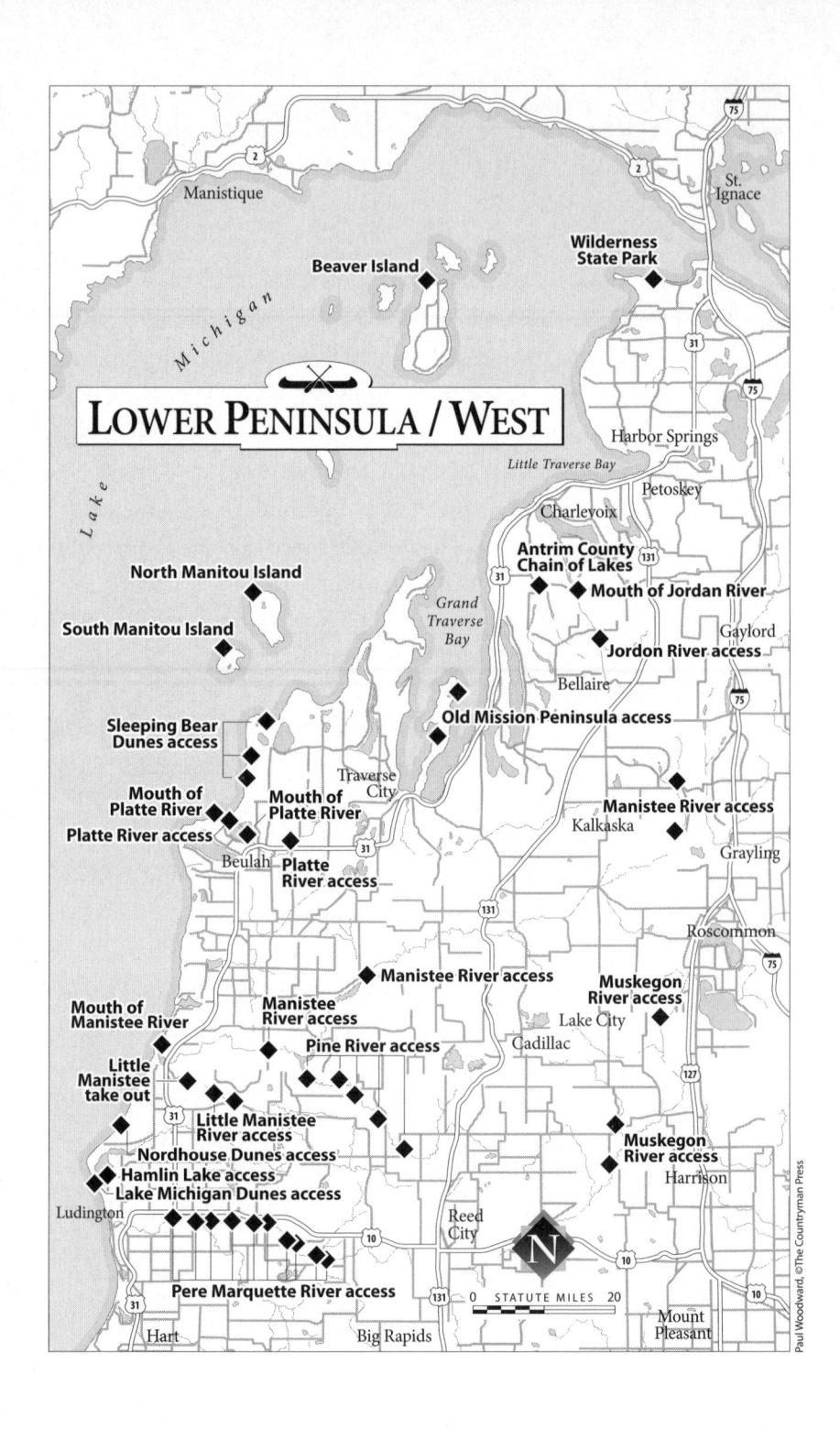

LOWER PENINSULA / WEST

Manistique

Beaver Island

Wilderness
State Park

St.
Ignace

Harbor Springs

Little Traverse Bay

Petoskey

Charlevoix

North Manitou Island

South Manitou Island

Antrim County
Chain of Lakes

Mouth of Jordan River

Jordon River access

Gaylord

Old Mission Peninsula access

Bellaire

Sleeping Bear
Dunes access

*Grand
Traverse
Bay*

Michigan

Lake

Mouth of
Platte River

Mouth of
Platte River

Traverse
City

Manistee River access

Kalkaska

Grayling

Platte River access

Beulah

Platte
River access

Manistee River access

Muskegon
River access

Roscommon

Mouth of
Manistee River

Manistee
River access

Pine River access

Lake City

Cadillac

Little
Manistee
take out

Little Manistee
River access

Nordhouse Dunes access

Muskegon
River access

Hamlin Lake access

Lake Michigan Dunes access

Harrison

Ludington

Reed
City

Pere Marquette River access

N

0   STATUTE MILES   20

Hart

Big Rapids

Mount
Pleasant

3 — Northwest Lower Peninsula

Jordan River, Antrim County Chain of Lakes, Platte River, Manistee River, Little Manistee River, Pine River, Pere Marquette River, Boardman River, Muskegon River; Lake Michigan

THIS REGION OF THE STATE is more populated than the northeast and has more private land, but there are good paddling opportunities, especially on the sprawling Manistee and Pere Marquette rivers. Lake Michigan offers sea kayaking opportunities—especially in the Grand Traverse Bay, along the Sleeping Bear Dunes and Nordhouse Dunes, and near Ludington.

If you're looking to spend quality paddling time with fine restaurants and accommodations within a short drive, this is the region for you. Traverse City is a major tourist destination, with many fine restaurants there and in the area. Bed & breakfasts abound, and there is top-quality lodging in hotels and resorts. Other towns with quality services are Cadillac, Manistee, and Ludington.

If You Had Five Days . . .

Day 1: Although the Sleeping Bear Dunes are better known, the Nordhouse Dunes south of Manistee offer a certain charm, and there are fewer visitors. Stay in either Manistee or Ludington.

Day 2: The Pere Marquette is better known for its fly-fishing, but it's a good river to paddle from Baldwin to Scottville. The starting point is Baldwin. There is lodging there, but paddlers looking for more upscale places should head to Ludington.

Day 3: The Sleeping Bear Dunes northwest of Traverse City are best seen on a sea kayaking trip in Lake Michigan. Traverse City offers top-notch accommodations and dining, but check out Leland, Glen Arbor, Empire, and the Leelanau Peninsula.

Days 4 and 5: A trip to Beaver Island via a ferry boat from Charlevoix will put you 32 miles out in the lake and on a sandy island perfect for kayaking. There's an outfitter on the island.

---

18. Jordan River

Best Runs: Graves Crossing to East Jordan
Accessibility: Good
Skill Level: Beginner to intermediate
Best Times: May to Oct.
Description: A gentle, short river leading to Lake Charlevoix
Home Base: East Jordan
Location: Northwest, east of US 131, on MI 66

THIS GENTLE PADDLE would make a good afternoon trip with children or for a couple looking to spend a few relaxing hours on a river during a vacation. With the surrounding hardwoods, it would make a good autumn color tour. It's served by an outfitter, so it would make a decent causal paddle while in the area.

I've fly-fished and paddled the Jordan for more than 30 years, and keep coming back—not just for the fishing, but for the beauty of the area. Unlike other northern Michigan rivers, it doesn't attract a lot of attention from paddlers—and apart from one campground, it's usually quiet.

The river is generally paddled from Graves Crossing Road, where the campground is located, to East Jordon. Upstream from Graves Crossing the river is too shallow, and the bottom filled with downed trees, to make paddling a comfortable experience.

Anglers could spend an entire day making the float while going after the rainbow, brook, and brown trout of the area.

Graves Crossing to Lake Charlevoix (10 miles, 4–5 hours): Clear water, tight turns

Put in at either Graves Crossing or the campground. The river is fast, 30–40 feet wide, and depths vary from 1 foot to drop-offs of up to 5 feet. It's generally a relaxing paddle, but you need to stay alert for turns. The river eventually slows as it nears Lake Charlevoix and eventually becomes still water through marshlands. There's a public access point beyond the MI 32 bridge in the land—it's on the left. There are other take-out spots at Webster and Rogers roads.

19. Antrim County Chain of Lakes

Best Runs: 12 lakes in the Upper and Lower Chains
Accessibility: Fair
Skill Level: Beginner to intermediate
Best Times: May to Oct.
Description: A series of gentle lakes and channels
Home Base: Ellsworth, Bellaire, Central Lake
Location: Northwest, between US 31 and MI 66, north of MI 72

THIS PADDLE ISN'T backcountry travel, and takes paddlers on a four-day trip with stops at elegant bed & breakfasts and top-notch restaurants. Paddlers can do various sections of the trip if they have limited time.

This trip takes paddlers through Michigan's "cottage country," where the shorelines have cottages and summer homes worth seeing— and they're best viewed from the water, where an observer can slow down and take in their various styles. The "cottage country" towns have a casual feel, but the lodging and eating out options are upscale.

Here's a general itinerary, but paddlers could plan various trips based on time and where they wanted to stay.

- Six Mile to St. Clair lakes (7 miles, 4–5 hours): Day 1
- Ellsworth to Intermediate lakes (16 miles, 6–8 hours): Day 2
- Bellaire Torch lakes (10 miles, 5–6 hours): Day 3
- Torch Lake to Elk Lake (16 miles, 6–8 hours): Day 4

Access

Six Mile Lake, Echo Township Park (www.antrimcounty.org/boat launch.asp), off Six Mile Lake Road; in Ellsworth, St. Clair–Six Mile Lake Natural Areas, from Ellsworth take CR 48 east about 2 miles to South Arm Township Park, where there's a launch; Torch Lake, Torch Lake Drive Boat Ramp, located 5 miles south of east port on US 31, to Barns Road, turn toward east, the ramp is 1 mile.

Outfitters

Jordan Valley Outfitters (231-536-0006; www.jvoutfitters.com), 311 N. Lake St., East Jordan. Provides canoes/kayaks to paddlers on the Jordan River and Chain of Lakes in Antrim County.

20. Platte River

Best Runs: Platte Lake to Lake Michigan
Accessibility: Fair
Skill Level: Beginner to intermediate
Best Times: May to Oct.
Description: Narrow in the upper portion, wide and deep in the lower stretch
Home Base: Honor

THE PLATTE IS A CLASSIC northern Michigan trout stream—with cold, clear, fast-running water that's easy to navigate (a good first river to introduce novices and children to the paddling sports).

It's easy enough so that a young person could be let loose on it in a small river kayak without worries about safety. Riding in a canoe with mom or dad can be boring in kids' terms, and this is the river to let them loose. There are several canoe/kayak outfitters in the area.

The river isn't deep, 2–4 feet at the most, and during dry summer months it can be much shallower. I fly-fish the river a lot, and the water is rarely over my knees.

The water can be fairly swift—the river drops 12.9 feet per mile, and kids can have a fun ride.

US 31 Bridge to MI 22 Bridge (12 miles, 5–6 hours): Forest lands, a lake to paddle

The river can be paddled upstream of Veteran's Memorial Campground at MI 31, but don't try it. The state maintains a fish hatchery near the bridge, and you can't portage around it. I tried it once, the workers there wouldn't allow it. The bottom is gravel and there are fallen logs that may be obstructions during low-water periods. The Platte River Campground, about an hour downstream, makes for a good stopping spot. It's on the right, but it's difficult to find. The river widens and there are riffles in the campground area. Most of the riverside is public land, but you'll see more development the closer you get to Honor, where there are two bridges. Your best bet is to paddle across Platte Lake, about 2.5 miles, and get out at the Platte River Campground just below MI 22. (See Sleeping Bear Dunes for MI 22 to Lake Michigan.)

21. Manistee River

> **Best Runs:** Near Grayling to Lake Michigan, 96 miles, 4–6 days
> **Accessibility:** Good
> **Skill Level:** Beginner to intermediate
> **Best Times:** May to Oct.
> **Description:** Narrow in the upper portion, wide and deep in the lower stretch
> **Home Base:** Grayling and Manistee
> **Location:** The headwaters form near Grayling and the river extends west and southwest to the city of Manistee on Lake Michigan.

AT 232 MILES, the Manistee is the second-longest river in Michigan, and provides trout fishing and paddling from its headwaters in Antrim County until it reaches Manistee Lake outside the city of Manistee on Lake Michigan.

Like most rivers in northern Michigan, it was used by loggers in the late-19th and early-20th centuries to float logs to lumber mills downstream, and many of those old white pines are still at the bottom of the river, providing cover for trout and obstacles for paddlers.

The Upper Manistee near Grayling can be paddled, but has tight turns. I've seen people on it in canoes and larger kayaks, but I'd opt for a small river kayak when paddling above MI 72. Below the highway, the river widens and deepens—larger boats can then be used.

Paddling the river's length is a good choice for those looking at extended trips. River access is good and there is plenty of public land to camp on. Road access is good, giving people the option to take one-, two-, or three-day trips.

The river winds through a fairly unpopulated area, where lodging is mostly found in small roadside mom-and-pop motels—and there's a scarcity of restaurants. If you're looking for big-town amenities, head to Grayling, Cadillac, or Manistee. If you're looking for a halfway-decent meal, head to the place where the pickup trucks are parked.

Deward to MI 72 (14 miles, 6–8 hours): Fly anglers, quality water

The river can be paddled from Deward, a long-gone lumber town, but access is better at Cameron Bridge or off County Road 612 (CR 612) at Red Bridge. Parking is tight at both bridges, where fly anglers often park. For a quality experience, put in at the Upper Manistee River State Forest Campground on Goose Creek Road, north of MI 72. Parking is easy and there's camping.

Those looking to either fish or do an easy float with stops may want to make an overnight trip, starting at Cameron Bridge and making camp at the state forest campground. One suggestion would be to set up a camp—and then head upriver and float back, taking it easy and knowing your camp is waiting.

I suggest spending as much time as possible on this section of the river because there are few other paddlers. Traffic picks up at MI 72 where there is a canoe/kayak livery. This is quality water, with river widths of 30–40 feet and depths at 1–3 feet—though there are some deep holes. There are logjams, but little portaging is needed. Most of the riverbanks are public land, but there are homes and private property on occasion.

MI 72 Bridge to Civilian Conservation Corps (CCC) Bridge (14 miles, 5–6 hours): Lots of traffic

This is a congested float on weekends and much of the shoreline is private property, which keeps you in your boat. Fly anglers are plentiful. I'd skip this section on weekends and float from the CCC Bridge to Lower Sharon or to the MI 66 Bridge, both day trips. The river is 40–80 feet wide and can range from 1–4 feet deep. The only camping available is at the CCC Bridge, with the grounds located upstream of it.

CCC Bridge to West Sharon Road (9 miles, 3–5 hours): A great fall color tour

It's not as congested here, with fewer anglers and less private property. It would be a colorful fall float with the hardwoods. It's fast running and has rocks to avoid. A good paddling strategy would be to put in at MI 72, paddle quickly to the CCC Bridge, and gently float to West Sharon Road. There are two bridges here, Lower and Upper Sharon, with the lower about 1.5 miles downstream. Both offer access and parking.

Lower Sharon Bridge to MI 66 Bridge (9.5 miles, 3–4 hours): Slow and wide

There's some motorboat traffic, but there's little riverbank development, and the paddling is easy. Smithville Forest Campground near MI 66 offers good campsites, and there's a public launch facility.

MI 66 to US 131 (25 miles, 7–10 hours): For experienced paddlers

Make sure you can do the distance. There are two emergency take-out spots, Custer and Lucas roads. There's a take-out at Chase Creek Campground, shortening the trip by three hours. For those up for the paddle, there are great rewards—with the high banks filled with pine, maple, and birch, making it a fall foliage trip. Old US 131 State Forest Campground is 0.5 mile beyond US 131, an offers primitive camping and parking.

US 131 to Baxter Bridge (10 miles, 4 hours): Slow waters

This slow-running deep water is a harbinger of what's to come as the river moves toward an area with two power dams, Tippy and Hodenpyle. There's a campground at Baxter Bridge offering access and parking.

Baxter Bridge to Glengary Bridge (17.5 miles, 6 hours): Power dam backwaters

Unless you're intent on paddling the entire river, I'd skip this portion—the wide waters, 50–100 feet, slow due to the upcoming Hodenpyle Dam and are filled with sediment. Beyond MI 37, the river becomes an impoundment and is flat-water paddling for nearly 7 miles. There are access points at Glengary Bridge and at MI 115. Nearby Mesick offers basic supplies and a couple of restaurants and taverns, but not much more. There's a portage on the right at Hodenpyle Dam, but don't try this unless you're an experienced river paddler—you are required to carry your boat and gear over a long distance on a rough trail.

Hodenpyle Dam to Red Bridge (10 miles, 4 hours): Portage around Tippy Dam

Portaging can be hard, but thankfully not always

The float along this 80–100-foot-wide undeveloped section can take up to four hours if the water is low, but only a few if the power dam releases water and speeds things along. There is no set schedule for water discharge, but it's usually in the morning. The high cliffs along it have a few waterfalls. At Red Bridge the river widens into an impoundment for about 6 miles until it reaches Tippy Dam, where there's a portage on the north shore. Stay to the north here and don't wander into the Pine River, which feeds into the Manistee at the impoundment.

Tippy Dam to Bear Creek (14 miles, 5–7 hours): Anglers in fall and spring

This isn't my favorite part of the river. I'd avoid it in the fall when throngs of salmon anglers flock here to either fish from shore or in small boats. Spring brings the steelhead fishing circus. This means paddlers will be dodging hooks and lures. Tippy Dam offers camping and boat launch facilities.

From Tippy to Manistee Lake the river is wide and deep, several hundred feet across at times, and its flow increases when water is released from the dam. There are gentle bends in the river as it winds its way to the lake.

There's no formal access point at Bear Creek, and you'll have to scramble up and down the river's banks. The creek is a favorite trout fishing spot for local anglers.

If you're paddling the entire river's length, you may want to try making it to Manistee Lake in a single paddling day that could last up to 10 hours.

Bear Creek to Manistee Lake (14 miles, 5–6 hours): Portage around fish weir

The last leg of the trip takes paddlers through more big waters and into Manistee Lake. I'd suggest ending your trip at either MI 55, where there is good access, or off US 31 in Manistee, where there are several boat launching sites. Manistee Lake is fairly industrial, and there are numerous plants located on it. You'll need to portage around a state fish weir 4 miles before getting to Manistee Lake.

Paddlers can get to Lake Michigan via the Manistee River Shipping Channel passing through the city, but be aware there are Great Lakes vessels passing through it—and its banks are walled, barring escape routes for paddlers.

22. Little Manistee River

Best Runs: Driftwood Valley to Stronach Park
Accessibility: Good

Skill Level: Intermediate to expert
Best Times: May to Oct.
Description: Tough little river
Home Base: Manistee, Wellston
Location: Northwest Michigan, off US 131, US 31, MI 55

THIS ISN'T THE RIVER for a first-time family outing—with its tight turns, fallen logs, and low water in the summer—and I suspect most use comes from trout anglers seeking secluded spots on the river. Spring and fall, the river is used by anglers after steelhead and salmon.

Although lesser known than its sibling to the north, the Little Manistee offers decent paddling for those interested in spending time on a smaller river. The river forms in Lake and Mason counties and runs through Manistee County before entering Manistee Lake.

Paddlers will compete for space on the river with anglers seeking trout, steelhead, and salmon. Also, paddling can be tricky—with tight turns and large logs in the water; during summer, water levels can get low.

If you're up for a real challenge and have expert skills, the 3-mile stretch of the river from 9 Mile Bridge (Campbell Road) to 6 Mile Bridge offers difficult conditions. Beginner to intermediate paddlers

A paddler negotiates the river

shouldn't even attempt the trip, as is noted in a warning from the U.S. Forest Service posted at 9 Mile Bridge.

Although the river can be paddled upstream from Indian Bridge off Irons Road near Irons to Driftwood Valley, I wouldn't suggest it for recreational paddlers. The river is narrow, and there are many fallen trees which require paddlers to get out of their craft and lift their boats over—a wet, soggy task.

A good Little Manistee starter paddler is from 6 Mile Bridge Road to Stronach Bridge on Old Stronach Road. The 4-mile paddle is through fairly fast-running water, with some challenging turns and a few logs to lift over. The water is 2–3 feet deep with deeper holes, and would be suitable for an intermediate paddler or beginner looking for a challenge.

Indian Bridge to Driftwood Valley (10 miles, 5–6 hours): Tough paddling, not suggested

Determined paddlers can put in at Indian Bridge off Irons Road. The river is narrow, 15–20 feet, and the water is shallow—especially in the summer; the low level further exacerbates the problem of trees across the river. An early spring trip would be the best to take advantage of the spring runoff, which makes the river deeper.

Driftwood Valley Campground to 9 Mile Bridge (Campbell Road) (9.5 miles, 3.5–5 hours): A moderate trip

This campground is the first real practical put-in on the river, and the trip takes paddlers along a classic Michigan trout stream with clear waters and a mostly undeveloped area of the river.

9 Mile Bridge to Stronach Road Bridge (11 miles, 5–7 hours): Difficult waters, not suggested

Hard-core paddlers looking for a challenge can put in at 9 Mile Bridge—but even for them, a small river kayak is the best choice of boats because they are easy to maneuver and lift over the many downed trees in this section. Recreational paddlers should look at putting in at 6 Mile Bridge.

Some obstacles you'll be confronted by are trickier than others

6 Mile Bridge Road to Stronach Bridge (6.5 miles, 3–4 hours): One portage, an easy float

The river widens and slows down, making the paddling easy, but there are still some logs across the river requiring paddlers to lift their craft over them. The water is fairly shallow, so it's not difficult. There are also a few narrow spots to maneuver through. The portage is around a state fish weir and is on the right, and not difficult. There are some large river homes on the stretch below the weir, but for the most part the river passes through public lands, much of it lowlands as the river nears its mouth at Manistee Lake. The paddle to the lake can be done, but it's better to take out at Stronach Bridge. Manistee Lake is surrounded by industrial facilities, and there is a shipping channel to contend with.

23. Pine River

Best Runs: Elm Flats to Peterson Bridge
Accessibility: Good
Skill Level: Beginner to intermediate
Best Times: May to Oct.
Description: Fast with some Class I and II rapids

Home Base: Manistee, Cadillac
Location: Northwest Michigan, off US 131, MI 55

THOSE ACCUSTOMED TO Michigan's mostly slow, meandering rivers will find a treat in the Pine, which runs fairly fast and has Class I and II white-water rapids, which is rare. The river has a National Wild and Scenic River designation and its 49-mile course has escaped intense development.

The river runs through Osceola, Lake, Wexford, and Manistee counties before emptying into the Manistee River system at the impoundment at Tippy Dam in Manistee County. It's a trout stream and paddlers will encounter some anglers.

There are also plenty of other paddlers, many attracted by its scenic river designation, its easy access off US 131 and MI 55, and its closeness to the Grand Rapids metro area. If you have your own boat, early morning paddles would help you avoid canoe traffic from the liveries. The upper river has less traffic.

Better accommodations will be found in nearby Cadillac or Manistee, but there are some in Wellston.

Gliding along a river

Skookum Road to Elm Flats (14 miles, 4.5–6 hours): Wide river, fallen logs

There are two public access points below Skookum Road off 6 Mile Road. The river is up to 45 feet wide and 1–4 feet deep. The water moves fairly quickly over the sandy gravel bottom and there are some fallen trees to handle.

Elm Flats to Peterson Bridge (12.5 miles, 4–5.5 hours): Whitewater, high banks

Michigan doesn't offer much whitewater, but paddlers will find it here. The Class I to II rapids can either be fun or daunting, depending on skill levels. Most with basic paddling skills can negotiate the rapids. Give yourself plenty of time to cover this stretch in case you want to stop before the rapids and check them out from the shore before running them. Dobson Bridge provides good access, with parking and public facilities. Watch out for large rocks in the river.

Peterson Bridge to Low Bridge (8 miles, 3–4 hours): Tricky waters, portage

This could be a rough float without intermediate paddling skills—it's not float-tub, family-friendly water. There's also a portage to the left around Stronach Dam. The water starts fairly fast and passes through narrow chutes, and there are challenging tight turns requiring good paddling skills, but it slows down as it approaches the dam. Low Bridge is about 20 minutes past the dam. For those who may be headed to the Manistee, there's a paddle through the backwaters of Tippy Dam (see Manistee River).

Outfitters

Pine River Paddlesports (231-862-3471; www.thepineriver.com), 9590 S. Grandview Hwy. S. MI 37, Wellston. Offers canoe and kayak rentals and trips, and has a campground. The center also has a livery at Walker Bridge where paddlers can put in and avoid some of the paddling traffic. It also offers car spotting services for paddlers with their own boats. Fees from $35–75.

Schomler Canoes and Kayaks (231-862-3475; www.schomier canoes.com), 11390 MI 37, Irons. This livery offers trips from two hours to three days on the Pine.

24. Pere Marquette River

Best Runs: The 42-mile stretch from Baldwin on MI 37 to Custer Bridge

Accessibility: Excellent, with put-ins and take-outs no further than four hours apart

Skill Level: Beginner to intermediate

Best Times: Late Apr. to Oct.

Description: The Pere Marquette is fairly wide, with easy-to-negotiate turns

Home Base: Baldwin

Location: Baldwin is on MI 37 in Lake County in the central portion of western Michigan

THIS RIVER IS what I call a great first-time paddling experience for those who want to get a taste of canoeing or kayaking. The river's flow is gentle enough for a first-time paddler to handle. It's generally wide in

Using one of the many access points before a day on the river

most spots, and although there are a few downed trees and boulders to navigate around, it's fairly easy; the river is rated for beginners and intermediates.

But while its gentle bends and turns are easy to negotiate, the river is a versatile paddling destination that offers various paddling options—including day and overnight trips that are easily arranged.

The river starts near Reed City and ends near Ludington (where it flows into Pere Marquette Lake), but it's the 42-mile stretch from MI 37 near Baldwin to Custer Bridge that receives the most attention from paddlers. That portion has been designated a National Wild and Scenic River, and most of its banks are in the Huron-Manistee National Forest—giving paddlers and anglers great access.

The best water to paddle is from the bridge at MI 37, 3 miles south of Baldwin, to Custer Bridge. However, most canoe liveries out of Baldwin don't extend their services past Walhalla Bridge, which makes that section one of the least paddled during the crowded summer months.

The Pere Marquette is well-marked for paddlers

The river is a versatile paddling destination that offers first-time paddlers a great place to get started. For veterans, it has various paddling options—including day and overnight trips, all of which can be easily arranged. The river is rated as an easy paddle. The water in most places can be waded.

During summer, the river is heavily used—especially on weekends when about 700 rental canoes and kayaks take to the waters, but with some planning you can avoid the crowds. Most paddlers go from the bridge at MI 37 to Gleason's Landing, gen-

A Perfect Day on the Pere Marquette . . .

8 AM: Breakfast at the Main Stream Café, MI 37, downtown Baldwin.

9 AM: A stop by the Pere Marquette Lodge fly shop to arrange for your trip and have your car spotted. There's coffee on hand and the staff there, including the fly-fishing guides, have a lot of river knowledge that they gladly pass along. The guides manage wooden drift boats in the river and know every hazard and downed tree.

10 AM: Get in the river at Gleason's Landing for a nearly five-hour float to Rainbow Rapids.

11 AM: Take a break along the shore for coffee and picture taking.

12 PM: Lunch break at Bowman's Bridge.

2 PM: Take a break to fly-fish in some of the deep holes. Hopefully brown trout are caught.

5 PM: Take out at Rainbow Rapids. There's a pretty steep hike up the hill to your car or the bus from the canoe livery.

6 PM: Back to your rented cabin at the Pere Marquette Lodge, where you cook steaks on the grills provided.

7 PM: A walk to the river, which is close by to watch the trout come up to feed on the evening insect hatchings. If you're a fly angler, this is a good time of day to try a bit more fishing.

8 PM: A night cap at Edie's Log Cabin bar in downtown Baldwin, about 3 miles north of the lodge on MI 37. It's the local hangout—if you don't want to cook, it's a good place for a burger and people watching.

10 PM: Lights out. After a day on the river, you're going to be pretty tired.

erally a four-hour trip. But you can also arrange to be dropped off farther downriver for a more solitary experience.

My preference is to use my kayak, so I can put in during the times of day I want to be on the river. That way I can enjoy the river without others around and indulge my other passion, fly-fishing. The cost is cheap, about $25 to have a service spot my vehicle. I use the Pere Marquette Lodge for this service. I simply give them my keys and tell them where I'm putting my boat in and where I'm getting out. A driver ferries my vehicle for me.

October is another peak time for river use, when anglers from

If You Had Three Days . . .

The estimated paddling time for floating the river from MI 37 in Baldwin to Custer Bridge is 15 to 18 hours, and a three-day trip would give you enough time to see the entire river. This could be done by either camping out two nights along the river or by floating various sections and staying in a motel.

Day 1: If you're planning on camping in the popular summer months, I'd suggest starting at Gleason's Landing and spending the night at Elk, which is only accessible by boat. This keeps the crowds at bay. If you're not camping, arrange to get out at the Upper Branch Landing, which is accessible by vehicle.

The landings are well marked, but you can miss them at night. Elk offers primitive camping and outdoor toilets. Make sure to bring drinking water, as not all landings have some on hand. The trip will take about six hours, depending on how fast you paddle. For an average paddler, this is enough time on the water—especially if you fish or sightsee along the way. The Elk access point is about 15 minutes past the Upper Branch Landing.

Day 2: If you're camping, the second day will be a long one—about eight hours on the water—but it's worth the effort because you'll be in a fairly unused section of the river. The trip takes you from the Upper Branch Landing to Custer Bridge, where there is primitive camping but no facilities. If you're not camping, I'd suggest getting out at either Walhalla Landing or Indian Bridge. The trip from the Upper Branch to Walhalla is about six hours.

Day 3: If you're really hard-core and want to make it from Custer to Ludington, you've got about four more hours of paddling ahead of you. Most folks get out at Scottville, which is only about an hour's paddle from Custer.

around the country head to the Pere Marquette for the annual salmon run. There's an almost festival feel to the river and the town of Baldwin during the season. The river can be paddled then, but be courteous to anglers who are stalking salmon. They've often invested a lot of time in one fish, and don't like to be disturbed. The best advice is to simply stop and ask the angler if it's all right to pass. It usually will be.

Paddlers will also encounter drift boats with anglers, especially in the "flies only" section of the river between MI 37 and Gleason's Landing, during most times of the year. Again, simply ask if it's okay to pass.

If you're just out for the pleasure of paddling, concentrate on trips between Gleason's Landing and Walhalla Bridge, where there are fewer anglers (and also paddlers) during summer. There are fewer summer homes along the river in that section, and more of a wilderness feeling.

Most of the riverbank along the Pere Marquette is public land belonging to either the Huron-Manistee National Forest Service or the state of Michigan, and there are many grassy banks to stop for a rest. Just make sure to respect the no trespassing signs. Cabins and summer homes tend to be clustered together on the river, so avoid stopping in such areas.

Most landings along the river offer camping, picnic tables, grills, and outhouses. These provide good places to stop for a lunch break. Most landings are no more than a couple of hours from each other.

Landing Information and Paddling Times

- M 37 to Green Cottage, 1 hour. You can launch a boat here, but there are no facilities.
- M 37 to Gleason's Landing, 3 hours from Green Cottage, 15 miles. The landing is on the right, where there are toilets, water, and tent camping.
- Bowman's Landing (1 hour from Gleason's Landing), 1 hour, 5 miles. The landing is on the left, and it offers water, toilets, and camping. A fee is charged.
- Bowman's Landing to Rainbow Rapids, 2.5 hours, 10 miles. The landing is on the right, but there is no camping. There are toilets on top of the hill.
- Rainbow Rapids to Sulak, 1 hour, 5 miles. The landing is on the left, there are toilets, and camping is allowed.
- Sulak to Upper Branch Landing, 1 hour, 5 miles. The landing is on the left and there are toilets and water.
- Upper Branch Landing to Elk, about 15 minutes, 0.5 mile. Elk is

accessible only by boat, and offers toilets, fire rings, and camping. There is no fee.

- Elk to Lower Branch Landing, 2 hours, 10 miles. The landing is on the left, but there are no facilities.
- Lower Branch Landing to Logmark, 1 hour. There are toilets but no other facilities.
- Logmark to Walhalla, 1.5 hours, 5 miles. The landing is past the bridge on the left, and it offers toilets but no other facilities.
- Walhalla to Indian Bridge, 1.5 hours, 8 miles. There are toilets and a boat ramp, but no other facilities.
- Indian Bridge to Custer, 1.5 hours, 8 miles. There is primitive camping available, but no facilities.
- Custer to Scottville, 1 hour, 6 miles. Camping is available in the city park, which offers toilets and water. There is a fee.
- Scottville to Ludington, 4 hours, 20 miles.

Fees

If you're planning on parking your vehicle in a lot managed by the Huron-Manistee Federal Forest Service, a user permit is required. The cost is $30 annually, $15 weekly. From late May to early September, a $2 per day boat permit is required. Permits are available at the Forest Service office, 650 N. Michigan Ave., Baldwin, 49304. Hours are from 9 AM–4:30 PM daily from mid-May through mid–September; winter, Monday through Friday.

Outfitters

Baldwin Canoe Rental (1-800-272-3642; www.baldwincanoe.com), 9117 S. M 37, Baldwin. Open from May through October. Prices from $45–110 for canoe/kayak rentals. Trips past Walhalla Bridge are subject to additional charges.

Ivan's (231-745-3361; www.ivanscanoe.com), 7332 S. MI 37, Baldwin. Ivan's offers rental watercraft, a campground, and cabins. Accommodations range from rustic campsites to facilities for RVs and cabins. Camping rates are $12 per site and up; cabins, $45–55.

25. Boardman River

Best Runs: Forks Campground to Boardman Pond
Accessibility: Good, with take-outs at camp grounds and bridges
Skill Level: Beginner to intermediate
Best Times: Late Apr. to Oct.
Description: The river can be narrow at places, some fallen trees
Home Base: Traverse City
Location: South of MI 72 in Traverse City along River Road

THE RIVER IS IN the heart of the Grand Traverse region, a top travel spot in Michigan, and is a popular destination for families. The river is well-used by trout anglers, and paddlers vie for space on the river with them.

There are a couple of days of paddling on the river, traveling 27 miles from the confluence of the North Branch and South Branch of the Boardman to Boardman Lake in Traverse City.

Forks Campground to Brown Bridge Dam (6 miles, 2–4 hours); Narrow river, downed trees

The put-in is at Forks Campground, which has good road access from Boardman Road. The river is mostly undeveloped here and passes through forestlands with some hardwoods, making for a good fall color tour. The river is fairly narrow, 25–30 feet, and the water levels can be low during the hot summer months, so you may have to get out of your canoe/kayak and pull it at times. Shreck's Place Campground is about halfway through the paddle, and would make a good lunch stop. The river moves

Paddlers on a warm afternoon in northern Michigan

into Brown Bridge Pond, where the water slows. The portage around Brown Bridge Dam is to the left.

Brown Bridge Dam to Beitner Road Bridge (6 miles, 2–4 hours): Beware of footbridges

You're starting to get into cottage country here—there are a large number of footbridges over the river that require some fancy paddling and sometimes ducking to avoid hitting your head. I favor a canoe in this stretch because there's more room to maneuver in one than in a kayak. The river widens up to 50 feet, but there are few places to take a break because of private property. It's best to terminate your trip at Beitner Road to avoid Beitner Rapids, a Class II rapid that runs for about 0.5 mile.

26. Muskegon River

Best Runs: Forks Campground to Boardman Pond
Accessibility: Good, with take-outs at campgrounds and bridges
Skill Level: Beginner to intermediate
Best Times: Late Apr. to Oct.
Description: The river can be narrow at places, some fallen trees
Home Base: Traverse City
Location: South of MI 72 in Traverse City along River Road

IT'S THE SECOND-LONGEST river in the state at 240 miles, and it provides recreation to people from the popular Houghton/Higgins lakes resort area to the industrial city of Muskegon on Lake Michigan.

The river is wide, warm, and deep, attracting paddlers and those in float tubes through much of its course. Along the way there are numerous canoe/kayak liveries, and countless access points. But as with many of Michigan's major rivers, it's really a series of rivers divided by power dams that produce similar impoundments that are themselves destinations for anglers, boaters, and campers.

The river is many things to many people, from an easy afternoon trip on a float tube to a multiday camping trip. It would also make a good first river for a family paddling trip, as there are many easy emer-

Paddling on a calm river

gency access points and the paddling could be done by a novice. There are many formal and informal campsites along the river.

There are two distinct rivers, the upper and lower Muskegon. The upper is more suited to overnight camping; the lower portion contains many dams and is heavily fished, especially for steelhead.

I have to admit, this isn't my favorite Michigan river because it's slow in many stretches, almost like flat water, and the scenery (although it's wooded) isn't the best. There are some portions in the Upper Muskegon that are worth paddling.

M 55 to Cadillac Bridge Road (10 miles, 4–6 hours): Family trip

There are several canoe liveries in this area, and it's a good family trip either by canoe or float tube. There are some fallen trees, but they're easy to negotiate because the river moves slowly through forested lowlands.

Cadillac Road to Leota Bridge (20 miles, 8–10 hours): A long day on a slow river

This float is about twice as long as most people want to be on the water, but it's not difficult, and you can make time with vigorous paddling.

The river is up to 60 feet wide and 6 feet deep at various places, but there are few obstacles and paddlers can make good time.

Church Bridge Road to MI 115 (10 miles, 4–5 hours): Easy trip, weekend crowds

There's a reason for the popularity of this stretch; it's a good one to do with kids on a summer weekend, as the river is up to 100 feet wide and shallow. It's a good one for a kid on a float tube. It's so shallow during summer that you may have to drag your canoe.

MI 66 Bridge to Evart (10 miles, 4–5 hours): Afternoon float

There's not much work to do on this stretch of the river, as it gently meanders through rolling farmlands. It's a good trip for couples with kids and could easily be done in an afternoon.

Lower Muskegon

There's a decent (but long) float between Evart and Big Rapids, 28 miles, but it could be cut short at Vance Road near the town of Hersey or at Hoover Road near Paris. The river widens to up to 200 feet in spots as it moves toward Big Rapids, where there is a dam to portage and Class I and II rapids to run (not recommended). From Big Rapids downstream to Muskegon the river goes through a series of power dams and their backwaters that aren't pleasant to paddle.

Outfitters

White Birch Canoe Trips & Camping (231-328-4547; www.whitebirch canoe.com), 4 miles west of Houghton Lake on MI 55, turn south on Jeff Road. A campground with kayaks/canoes and tubes for rent.

    River Country Campground (231-734-3808; www.campandcanoe .com), 6281 River Rd., Evart. Campgrounds and watercraft rentals.

Lake Michigan

Beaver Island, Old Mission Peninsula, Nordhouse Dunes/Ludington State Park, Sleeping Bear Dunes National Lakeshore, Wilderness State Park

FOR SEA KAYAKERS, this region offers tremendous potential, with hundreds of miles of Lake Michigan shoreline to explore—much of it along sand dune areas, and with islands to visit that are destinations in themselves.

Much of the lake shore is public land, from state parks to the Sleeping Bear Dunes National Lakeshore, so access is excellent. The region offers some of Michigan's better upscale accommodations and fine dining. In the middle of it is the Grand Traverse vineyard area, and one enterprising kayak guide has started offering kayak winery tours out of the Traverse City area.

Negotiating the waters of Lake Michigan

If You Had Five Days . . .

Day 1: Head to the Sleeping Bear Dunes National Lakeshore near the town of Empire. Stop at the visitors center for information and a map, and then head out on Lake Michigan for a tour of the dunes.

Day 2: Wilderness State Park, tucked away in the outskirts of this region, is a little-used place where paddlers could spend days exploring the shoreline.

Days 3 and 4: A trip to Beaver Island out of Charlevoix is a commitment, but its reward is a remote island to paddle that has lodging and restaurants.

Day 5: A paddle on Old Mission Peninsula offers views of the cherry orchards and vineyards for which the area is known.

---

27. Beaver Island

Best Runs: Trip around island
Accessibility: Good
Skill Level: Beginner to intermediate
Best Times: May to Oct.
Description: Warm waters of Lake Michigan, sandy shores
Home Base: Beaver Island
Location: Northwest, Lake Michigan, offshore from Charlevoix

THIS ISLAND IS the largest island in Lake Michigan and is a 32-mile boat ride from Charlevoix on the mainland in northwest Michigan. It (and the several islands surrounding it) is a great destination for sea kayakers.

The island has a colorful history and was home to the only kingdom established in America. It started when a Morman leader, James Strang, arrived on the island in 1848 with a group of followers. They came from Wisconsin to avoid persecution, and they built cabins and established farms. Strang became involved in politics and served in the Michigan legislature. In 1850 he proclaimed himself king of his followers, which included most of the island's residents.

Clashes ensued between him and nonbelievers, and even with members of the sect. Strang was eventually killed by two men in 1856 as he walked toward the U.S.S. *Michigan*, a naval gunboat to which he had been invited. The men reportedly ran to the ship and were never seen again. Strang's followers were driven off the island shortly after by groups of citizens from Mackinac and St. Helena islands.

The pace is much less hectic these days, and tourism has replaced farming as the major industry on the island, home to about three hundred year-round residents.

For paddlers, the warm waters of Lake Michigan provide many possible excursions around the island and the more than dozen surrounding ones.

If you're new to paddling, this would be a great place to learn. The Inland Seas School of Kayaking has a good track record of teaching (see *Outfitters* below).

Summer water temperatures in the 60s and the white, sandy beaches on the island's shoreline make it an easy paddle, even for beginners. Recreational kayakers will have no trouble negotiating the shoreline or even paddles to the outlying islands, so long as they have self-rescue skills.

For starters, try a trip around St. James Harbor or Little Sand Bay. A more challenging trip would be over to Garden Island and back—a full day (about 10 miles) of paddling, with a little exploring of the outer island. A trip around the island is about 40 miles and would take about four days if there are no problems with the weather. Much of the land is open to wilderness, low-impact camping.

Access

Beaver Island Boat Co. (231-547-2311 or 1-888-446-4095; www.bibco .com), 103 Bridge Park Dr., Charlevoix. Open April to December, the boat makes two to four trips weekly. The 32-mile trip to the island takes about two hours. It's best to call ahead for reservations if you're transporting a canoe/kayak. The cost per vehicle for a round-trip ranges from $150–180, depending on the size. Canoes/kayaks on top of vehicles are free (unless they make the vehicle taller than 7 foot 6 inches, then there's an additional charge). The cost of transporting a canoe/ kayak not on a vehicle is $44 round-trip.

Outfitters

Inland Seas School of Kayaking (231-448-2221; www.inlandsea kayaking.com), P.O. Box 437, Beaver Island, 49782. This school handles lessons for beginners through experts, and also offers day and extended trips around the island.

28. Old Mission Peninsula

Best Runs: Bowers Harbor tour
Accessibility: Fair
Skill Level: Beginner to intermediate
Best Times: May to Oct.
Description: Peninsula in the protected waters of Grand Traverse
    Bay, Lake Michigan
Home Base: Traverse City
Location: MI 37 north of Traverse City

THE PENINSULA OFFERS 40 miles of shoreline covered with orchards and vineyards on its low-lying hills, but access is limited to three put-in places—Bowers Harbor, Old Mission Lighthouse, and Haserot Beach.

Traverse City is one of the state's top tourist destinations, with a growing number of wineries drawing wine buffs with tours. One enterprising kayak guide service has even put together a kayak winery tour.

Traverse City, with its many fine restaurants and upscale accommodations, would make a great place from which to explore much of northwest Michigan by canoe or kayak. Day trips could be made to the Sleeping Bear Dunes (see Sleeping Bear Dunes National Lakeshore in this section) for sea kayaking trips or to the Manistee River (see Manistee River in the previous section) for river trips.

Two islands, Power and Bassett, can be visited by kayakers from Bowers Harbor. Power Island has trails, and Bassett Island has five primitive campsites. They're usually crowded—to make reservations, contact the Grand Traverse Parks and Recreation Department.

Access

Old Mission Lighthouse: Take US 37 from Traverse City north about 18 miles to the tip of the peninsula. Parking is available.

Bowers Harbor: The boat launch is on Neh-ta-wanta Road about 8 miles north of Traverse City via US 37. Take Seven Hills Drive to the left and make a left on Neh-ta-wanta.

Haserot Beach: The launch is on Swaney Road on the northern tip of the peninsula. Take US 37 about 14 miles north, and make a right on Swaney.

Resources

Grand Traverse Parks and Recreation (231-922-4818; www.co.grand -traverse.mi.us/departments/parks_rec), 1213 W. Civic Center Dr., Traverse City. Call for reservations for Bassett Island campsites.

29. Nordhouse Dunes/Ludington State Park

> **Best Runs:** Ludington State Park to Nordhouse Dunes, 11 miles, 6 hours
> **Accessibility:** Fair
> **Skill Level:** Beginner to intermediate
> **Best Times:** May to Oct.
> **Description:** Open waters of Lake Michigan
> **Home Base:** Manistee/Ludington
> **Location:** Lake Michigan between Ludington and Manistee, off US 31

THE 3,450-ACRE DUNES and Ludington State Park area has 12 miles of undeveloped Lake Michigan shoreline; along with Hamlin Lake, paddlers could spend several days in the area.

The Nordhouse Dunes are lesser known than the Sleeping Bear Dunes, but provide a view for paddlers that has been pretty much unchanged since the coming of the first Europeans, with dunes up to 140 feet high.

It's a great paddling destination because you can either go on the big waters of Lake Michigan for a dunes tour or see them from Hamlin Lake, which is my personal favorite. The lake is formed by the Big Sable River. There's good camping in the state park, and Ludington and Manistee offer lodging, restaurants, and shopping.

For families, the area provides great days on the undeveloped beaches and Hamlin Lake is a good place to introduce kids to paddling—

it's warm and calmer than Lake Michigan. Nearby, the Pere Marquette, Manistee, and Little Manistee rivers provide river paddling.

Lake Michigan Recreation Area to Ludington State Park (8–11 miles, 5–6 hours): Dunes and a lighthouse

The dunes stretch out, giving a paddler the feeling they've gone back in time—no signs of human habitation, just 50-foot dunes with wild grasses waving in the breeze. It's a gentle, unhurried trip, with breaks taken on the beach. In the middle of the paddle is Big Sable Point Lighthouse, dating from the 19th century. A paddle to the light and back to your vehicle at the recreation area would make for a 12-mile trip—a full paddling day. Another few hours brings you to Ludington State Park, where MI 116 provides good access to a take-out.

Hamlin Lake (12 miles, 5 hours): A good kid's paddle, warm swimming water

The lake can be paddled in almost any kind of boat, especially if you stay near shore. It's a favorite of mine. Put in at the boat launch facility near the concession stand. On warm summer weekends you're going to be contending with powerboaters and sailboats for space, but once on the water it's worth the effort. There is some motorboat traffic, but stay to the west side of the lake where it's mostly public lands and you'll find less traffic. Head north toward the dunes, but look for small channels to the west leading to Hidden Lake—a serene body of calm water little-visited by motorboat traffic. There are small inlets to explore and the shoreline is undeveloped. A good paddler in a fast boat can make the trip to the dunes and back to the launch in less than three hours, but schedule more time for the trip so you can swim and sunbathe there.

Access

Two spots provide access in the dunes area, the Lake Michigan Recreation Area and Ludington State Park off MI 116, 5.5 miles north of Ludington. The best access is from Ludington State Park, either from MI 116 (which runs to the park) or from the park itself. It's less than 50 yards from the road to the water. Access from the Lake Michigan Recreation

Area at Nordhouse Dunes is extremely difficult; it's about a 100-yard boat carry from the parking lot and it involves a series of steps. There is nowhere nearby where you can simply drag your boat to the water—you're going to need at least two people or more to carry your boat.

30. Sleeping Bear Dunes National Lakeshore

Best Runs: Lake Michigan coastline, Platte and Crystal rivers, inland lakes, 35 miles
Accessibility: Good
Skill Level: Beginner to intermediate
Best Times: May to Oct.
Description: Open waters of Lake Michigan
Home Base: Empire, Frankfort, Honor, and Traverse City
Location: Northwest, Grand Traverse region, off MI 22

THE SLEEPING BEAR DUNES National Lakeshore offers a diversity of paddling experiences, ranging from several-hour river trips for kids and first-time paddlers to challenging sea kayak trips on Lake Michigan and near north and south Manitou Islands.

A family can find many things to do here in the prime travel destination of the Grand Traverse region, including camping and swimming. There are also historical exhibits in Glen Haven, including a general store, blacksmith shop, and wooden boat museum.

The dunes are the central attraction, and paddling is the best way to see them. For kids, there's an easy river paddle that takes them on the Platte River to a Lake Michigan beach.

Nearby Traverse City, Glen

Near the Sleeping Bear Dunes on Lake Michigan

Paddler dwarfed by the dunes

Arbor, and Empire offer travelers many opportunities to dine in up-scale restaurants and enjoy diverse lodging options—ranging from chain motels to resorts to bed & breakfasts. The region has a large number of wineries to tour.

For advanced paddlers, north and south Manitou Islands in Lake Michigan offer wilderness trips and camping. Some brave souls make the crossing from Glen Haven to South Manitou—nearly 8 miles and 2–3 hours away. A better bet is to take the ferry from Leland to either island and avoid the open water crossing.

Platte River Paddle

If you're looking for an easy paddle to get kids interested in the sport, this is one of the best places in the state. The river could be paddled in one 8 hour trip, or broken down into two short trips.

The most exciting one for kids takes paddlers along the Platte River from MI 22 to Lake Michigan and takes 2–3 hours. With time at the beach, and lunch, paddlers with kids could make a day of it.

For a longer trip, put in at Veteran's Memorial State Forest Campground off US 31 east of Honor and float the river to Platte Lake and across it to MI 22, where you could either take out or continue on to Lake Michigan.

(Lake Michigan) Glen Haven to Esch Road (11 miles, 8 hours): *Sand dunes and nude beaches*

The nude beaches start about 1 mile north of the put-in. It's not a formal area; it's just that they're usually found there. The park service is pretty lax about enforcement, so it's pretty laissez-faire. The paddle soon takes you to the Empire Bluffs, some of the highest dunes. A good stop is at North Bar Lake, where a stream runs into the big lake—a popular swimming spot. The Pierce Stocking Scenic Drive is a midway point, and the dunes are large. The big dunes prevail until you get close to the end, Glen Haven, which has a historical village including a Coast Guard station and old boat museum. There's great view here of the Manitou Islands.

(Lake Michigan) Glen Haven Bohermian Road (11 miles, 8 hours): *Private property and dunes*

There's a lot of private beachfront here, so don't bother stopping until the mouth of the Crystal River. The Homestead Resort is just north, and is also private beachfront. Here the condos tower, not the dunes. Further north are more dunes with public access, but unless you're in

---

A Perfect Day at the Sleeping Bear Dunes . . .

8 AM: Breakfast at the Crescent Bakery on Main Street in Frankfort. It's known for its handcrafted pastries.

9 AM: Put in kayak at the Esch Road Beach, paddle north along the dunes, stopping along the way to view them and swim.

11 AM: Arrive at the public beach in Empire for a stroll to stretch your legs after a long paddle.

12 PM: A picnic lunch on the beach.

1 PM: Put back in the water and head south back to your vehicle. Take a few breaks to stroll on the sandy beaches.

3 PM: Arrive back at Esch Road Beach and head toward Glen Arbor.

4 PM: Check into one of the bed & breakfasts.

6 PM: Dinner at the cozy Art's Tavern in downtown Glen Arbor.

8 PM: Head west 2 miles on MI 109 to Glen Haven and put the kayak into Lake Michigan for a moonlight tour of Sleeping Bear Bay.

The Sleeping Bear Dunes have a lot to offer

training for an iron man contest, I wouldn't suggest trying to climb them. Past that you enter Good Harbor Bay, with more private property.

Checking In and Fees

Before padding in the dunes area, stop at the Philip A. Hart Visitors Center in Empire. Various daily and year-round passes are required for parking and use of the dunes area. The officials there are knowledgeable about paddling. If you're planning to make the 8-mile crossing on the open waters of Lake Michigan to either north or south Manitou Islands, the park service requires you to file a paddling plan so they can keep track of you. Also, if planning a kayaking/camping trip, paddlers are required to obtain backcountry camping permits from the park service.

Outfitters

Riverside Canoe Trips (231-325-5622; www.canoemichigan.com), MI 22 at the Platte River, Honor. Offers canoe/kayak rentals for trips on the upper and lower Platte River, and a spotting service for those with their own boats. Call ahead for reservations.

Crystal River Outfitters (231-334-4420; www.crystalriveroutfitters .com), 6249 W. River Rd., Glen Arbor. Rents canoes/kayaks and float tubes for four to five hour trips from Glen Lake to Lake Michigan via the Crystal River. They provide shuttle service for those with their own boats.

Resources

Philip A. Hart Visitors Center (231-326-5134; www.nps.gov/slbe /planyourvisit/visitorcenters), MI 72, just east of MI 22, Empire. Open daily from late May to early September, 8 AM–4 PM. The center is a good place to stop first no matter what you're planning to do. They have information about camping in the dunes, museums, fees, and restrictions on how the lakeshore can be used.

31. Wilderness State Park

Best Runs: Tours of Big Stone Bay and Sturgeon Bay
Accessibility: Excellent
Skill Level: Beginner to expert
Best Times: May to Oct.
Description: The Lake Michigan shoreline is mostly sandy; the sheltered bays can be calm, but you can run into rough seas, depending on the winds
Home Base: Mackinaw City
Location: Northwest tip of the Lower Peninsula, just minutes off I-75

THE PARK IS AN UNSPOILED paddling destination, located only 8 miles west of one of Michigan's most-visited places, Mackinaw City. A few days spent at the park offers some tremendous padding on Lake Michigan, including the sheltered Sturgeon Bay. There's also French Farm Lake nearby, offering paddling on an undeveloped body of water surrounded by state land.

This would be a good place to stay for those looking for a place to enjoy hiking, mountain biking, and paddling. The 10,512-acre park offers 26 miles of Lake Michigan beaches and 16 miles of trails for mountain bikers.

There are 250 modern campsites in two units, six rustic cabins, and three rustic bunkhouses for rent. There are boat launches, but many of the rustic cabins are on Lake Michigan, and you have your own section of the beach.

It's a short drive to Mackinaw City where there are plenty of shops, restaurants, and historic attractions.

Big Stone Bay (8–10 miles, 6 hours): Piping plovers, cobble beaches

Paddlers could make a day of this trip, which takes them along wide sandy beaches and forested dune areas. Look for the endangered piping plover, which finds its habitat on the cobble beaches. The trip around the bay is 8–10 miles, which is pretty much all one should paddle. An evening tour would enable you to watch the sun set over Lake Michigan.

Sturgeon Bay to Outer Islands (12 miles, 8 hours): Possible overnight trip

Put in off North Lake Shore Drive for a day trip on Sturgeon Bay. It's about 12 miles to the park's outer islands and back. Try a shorter trip to Goose Bay to explore the sandy inlets. The paddle would also make for a good overnight trip including backcountry wilderness camping. Check with the park office for permits.

In the Area

Lodging

ON BEAVER ISLAND (LAKE MICHIGAN)

Beaver Island Lodge (231-448-2396; www.beaverislandlodge.com), 38210 Beaver Lodge Dr. The 15-room lodge has standard motel-style rooms and suites, many with a view of the lake. Some suites offer a full kitchen. Nina's Restaurant is inside (see *Eating Out*). The innkeepers are Nina Simpson-Jones and Ray Cole. Rates from $65–145.

Emerald Island Hotel (231-448-2376; www.emeraldislandhotel .com), 37986 Kings Hwy. Open year-round. The hotel is fairly new and has 16 units. The efficiency units have two queen beds and a kitchen. The suites have two bedrooms and a kitchen and can sleep six. The rooms have cable TV and private baths. No pets and no smoking. Rates from $100–130.

IN EAST JORDAN (JORDAN RIVER, ANTRIM COUNTY CHAIN OF LAKES)

Jordan Inn (231-536-9906; www.jordaninn.com), 288 Main St., East Jordan, 49727. The inn has four suites and two rooms, all of which have a cottage feel and are decorated with furnishings ranging from French country to Victorian. Most rooms have king-sized beds, and some have a view of Lake Charlevoix. Rates from $90–125.

IN ELLSWORTH (ANTRIM COUNTY CHAIN OF LAKES)

The House on the Hill (231-588-6304; www.thehouseonthehill.com), 9661 Lake St., Ellsworth, about 20 minutes from Charlevoix. The seven-room B&B has rooms in the main house and a carriage house. All have private baths and are well decorated. I liked the carriage house rooms the best. All have private entrances and a view of the gardens. Rates from $175–200.

IN FRANKFORT (LAKE MICHIGAN, PLATTE RIVER)

Betsie Bay Inn (231-352-8090; www.betsiebayinn.com), 231 Main St., Frankfort. The Victorian-style inn has 17 rooms. The diversity of room style is refreshing, and you can select from a Victorian motif or more modern natural wood. Some rooms have hot tubs, saunas, and log stoves. There are queen- and king-sized beds. A restaurant and bar are available (see *Eating Out*). Rates from $105–255.

Stonewall Inn (231-352-9299), 428 Leelanau Ave., Frankfort. This Victorian Italianate home is the oldest in the area, built in 1860, and was for a while the Frankfort Land Co. It's on the National Register of Historic Places. There are four rooms decorated with antiques and Civil War memorabilia. I liked the feel of the place, with the Civil War sabers and uniforms. The Lincoln room has a 6-foot walnut headboard. Dave and Sandy Jackson are the innkeepers. Rates from $110–125.

IN GLEN ARBOR (LAKE MICHIGAN, PLATTE RIVER)

Glen Arbor Bed & Breakfast (231-334-6789; www.glenarborbnb.com), 6548 Western Ave., Glen Arbor. The six-room B&B is within walking distance of shopping and restaurants in Glen Arbor. The rooms are taste-fully decorated in a country Victorian style, and have air-conditioning and cable TV. There is a nice porch. It was built in 1873 and has been a boardinghouse for loggers, a restaurant, and a private home. There are also two guest cottages for rent. Room rates are from $89–185 and cot-tages are from $795–1,095 per week.

The Homestead (231-334-5100; www.thehomesteadresort.com), 1 Wood Ridge Rd., Glen Arbor. The Homestead is an older-style lodge that has gone upscale. It has become a near village and has various types of lodging available, ranging from hotel rooms to condos and homes for rent. There is a private beach and a restaurant and a children's center. There's an outside pool and tennis courts. Rates from $100 up.

IN LUDINGTON (NORDHOUSE DUNES/LUDINGTON STATE PARK)

Cartier Mansion Bed & Breakfast and Conference Center (231-843-0101; www.cartiermansion.com), 409 E. Ludington Ave., Ludington. The bed & breakfast was built in 1903 by a lumber baron, and there are five fireplaces, a black walnut library, and a mahogany music room. The six rooms have high-speed Internet. The Grand King Suite has a four-poster bed, sitting room, and large bath. Most of the rooms are larger than what many B&Bs have to offer in Michigan. Wedding friendly. Much of the original woodwork is intact, and various types of wood were used. Rates are $125–225.

Inn at Ludington (231-845-7055 or 1-800-845-9170; www.inn-ludington.com), 701 E. Ludington Ave., Ludington. There are six rooms in this 1890 Victorian-style mansion. All have private baths. While many B&Bs slavishly try making every room a replica of Victo-rian life, this inn has a different theme for each room, ranging from the classic Great Lakes Victorian Suite to the Scandinavian Room. A full breakfast is served, and there is Internet access. Rates from $90–165.

IN TRAVERSE CITY (GRAND TRAVERSE BAY, SLEEPING BEAR DUNES, PLATTE RIVER, BOARDMAN RIVER)

The Great Wolf Lodge (231-941-3600; www.greatwolflodge.com), 3575 US 31 North, Traverse City. This is a family place with lots of kids drawn there by a water park and a 52,000-square-foot indoor enter-tainment area. There are indoor and outdoor pools, restaurants, and arcades. The giant North Woods–style building has 281 rooms with TV, microwave, and refrigerator. Rates from $239–415.

Grey Hare Inn Vineyard Bed & Breakfast (231-947-2214; www.greyhareinn.com), 1994 West Rue de Carroll Rd., Old Mission Peninsula. This B&B is located on a working farm and vineyard and offers stays and wine tasting. There are three rooms, with a French farmhouse feel. One room has a hot tub. Rates from $135–250.

Wind in the Pines (231-932-8608; www.windinthepinesbb.com), 13573 S. Gallagher Rd., Traverse City. Located on 6 acres just west of downtown Traverse City, this three-room B&B is a real find in an urban environment. The rooms have an Up North feel, with natural-log paneling. They are sparsely furnished and clean, just the type of room you want to stay in after a day outdoors. A full breakfast is served daily in the dining room, which features a fireplace. The lower-level guest rooms have access to a separate ground-floor entrance. Rates from $100–125.

Neahtawanta Inn (1-800-220-1415; www.neahtawantainn.com), 1308 Neahtawanta Rd., Traverse City. Located on the Old Mission Peninsula in an 1885 cottage that has served as a summer hotel since 1906, the inn is near Grand Traverse Bay and is a great destination for kayakers. There are four rooms, plus a two-bedroom suite that has a small kitchen and a living room. Breakfasts are vegetarian. Rates from $105–260.

Traverse Bay Lodge (231-947-5436; www.traversebaylodge.com), 460 Munson Ave., Traverse City. This place is a step up from a normal motel, and it's comfortable and close to downtown Traverse City. The rooms are nothing special, but they are clean and serviceable. There is an indoor pool and spa and an exercise room. Rates from $59–209.

Ranch Rudolf (231-947-9529; www.ranchrudolf.com), 6841 Brownbridge Rd., Traverse City. Open year-round. The ranch offers 16 rooms and 25 campsites and is on the banks of the Boardman River, and would be a great home base for paddlers. The resort offers horseback riding, canoeing/tubing, and a restaurant. Rates from $78–185.

IN MANISTEE (MANISTEE RIVER, LITTLE MANISTEE RIVER, NORDHOUSE DUNES)

The Ramsdell Inn (231-398-7901; www.ramsdellinn.net), River and Maple streets, Manistee. The 10-room bed & breakfast is in a restored turn-of-the-century commercial building in the heart of the downtown area, not far from a boardwalk along the Manistee River. T. J.'s is a small tavern in the inn that offers pub food. Sporadic hours. Room rates from $109–200.

Manistee Inn & Marina (231-723-4000 or 1-800-968-6277; www.manisteeinn.com), 378 River St., Manistee. Located along the Manistee River in the downtown area, the inn has 25 rooms. They're basic hotel rooms, nothing special, but could be good if you're a boater coming in from several days on the lake—rooms can be within walking distance of your craft. It's also close to restaurants and shopping and has wireless Internet. The inn has 15 slips on the Manistee River and can accommodate boats up to 25 feet. Water and electric hook-ups are available. Rates from $90–150.

Riverside Motel & Marina (231-723-3554; www.riversidemotel andmarina.com), 520 Water St., Manistee. Open year-round. Rooms in this 20-unit motel are simple and sparse, but clean. Many have a view of the Manistee River and doors leading to the water. The rooms have phones and satellite TV. There are boat docks available, as well as a fish-cleaning station. There are lawn chairs, grills, picnic tables, and an outdoor pool. Rates from $89–139.

IN WELLSTON (PINE RIVER, LITTLE MANISTEE RIVER)

Coolwater on the Pine (231-862-3481; www.coolwatercamp.com), 9424 W. 48½ Rd., Wellston. Located on the river, this resort offers rustic campsites, cabins, and a trailer for rent. Rates from $24–32 for campsites, $65–70 for cabins.

Schmidt Outfitters (231-848-4191; www.schmidtoutfitters.com), 918 Seaman Rd., Wellston. This fly-fishing shop offers float trips on the Pine for anglers, and it has a small, upscale woody motel nearby with pine-paneled rooms and rustic décor suited for paddlers. The owner, Ray Schmidt, holds forth in the fly shop and is a wealth of information for anglers and paddlers. Rates from $75–100.

Lumber Jack Lodge (231-848-7777; www.lumberjack-lodge.com), 1957 Seaman Rd., Wellston. The rooms have private baths, pets are allowed, and there are fire pits. Rates from $50–60.

IN CADILLAC (PINE RIVER)

McGuire's Resort (1-800-634-7302; www.mcguiresresort.com), 7880 Mackinaw Tr., Cadillac. If you're looking for an upscale golf-course-style resort with a restaurant and lodging, this is the best near the Pine. The rooms are large and modern and some have hot tubs and fireplaces. There's a 27-hole golf course, pool, sauna, and hot tub. Rates from $80–100.

IN BALDWIN (PERE MARQUETTE RIVER)

The Pere Marquette River Lodge (231-745-3972, www.pmlodge.com), 8841 S. MI 37, on the banks of the Pere Marquette River. This venerable place has been a fixture on the river for decades, but in the past few years (under the ownership of Frank Willets) the rooms, cabins, and even two riverside homes that are rented out have been renovated and cleaned up. The log lodge offers simple one- and two-bedroom rooms, and there's a large common area with a fireplace and couches. There's a larger dining area that's used for conferences. Adjoining it is the lodge's fly-fishing shop, which also offers assorted gear for paddlers and drift-boat fishing trips for anglers. You don't need to fish on a drift boat trip. You can also use a trip, priced from $300 and up, for sightseeing. Riverside dinners are also offered on special occasions. The fly shop offers vehicle spotting services for paddlers who want to use their own boats. The cost is $25. Room rates from $80 and up for the cabins and homes.

    Red Moose Lodge (231-745-6667, www.redmooselodge.com), 8982 S. MI 37, on the banks of the Pere Marquette River. This would be a great starting point for a float trip as there's a canoe/kayak launch on the property. The owner, Clint Anderson, has renovated the nearly dozen rooms in a North Woods style. There's also a common area that offers wireless Internet service and coffee in the morning. The lodge also has a vehicle spotting service for patrons and Anderson offers guided fishing trips. Room rates from $70–85.

IN MACKINAW CITY (WILDERNESS STATE PARK, LAKE MICHIGAN)

The city offers a variety of accommodations ranging from chain hotels to bed & breakfasts.

Wilderness State Park (231-436-5381; www.michigan.gov/dnr), 903 Wilderness Park Dr., Carp Lake. The cabins fill up quickly and it's suggested that paddlers make reservations. The state Department of Natural Resources maintains a good Web site for reservations (www .midnrreservations.com).

Brigadoon of Mackinaw City (231-346-8882; www.mackinaw brigadoon.com), 207 Langlade St., Mackinaw City. Open from April to October. Innkeeper Sherree Hyde has a gem of a place tucked away on a side street. The eight suites are decorated in Victorian style and are spacious. Some rooms have separate sitting areas and bedrooms, and many have a view of Lake Huron. Rates from $165–255.

Deer Head Inn (231-436-3337; www.deerhead.com), 109 Henry St., Mackinaw City. Open year-round, this home has been turned into a small B&B with five outdoorsy-style rooms, including the Hemingway Room. Each has a private bath, fireplace, TV, and wireless Internet. The home is one of the oldest in town and was built in 1913 by a local banker, lumberman, and hotel owner. A full breakfast is served. Rates from $100–225.

Platte River Campground (1-877-444-6777; www.nps.gov/slbe /planyourvisit/platterivercamp), 10 miles south of Empire on the Platte River. The National Park Service campgrounds are very popular and are pretty much filled from late June until early September, so the park service suggests that paddlers make reservations several months ahead of time. The sites have good spacing between them, and you don't feel like you're being crowded. There are sites for large groups and water and showers are available.

D. H. Day Campground (231-326-5134; www.nps.gov/slbe/plan yourvisit/dhdaycamp), 8000 W. Harbor Hwy., Glen Arbor. These 88 sites are more rustic than the Platte River Campground, and there are only outhouse-type toilets and cold water from spigots, but the reward is that it's within walking distance of Lake Michigan beaches. The campground doesn't take reservations.

Eating Out

ON BEAVER ISLAND (LAKE MICHIGAN)

Nina's Restaurant (231-448-2396; www.beaverislandlodge.com), 38210 Beaver Lodge Dr. Open daily. Located in Beaver Island Lodge (see

Lodging). This place has the largest menu of any restaurant on the island, and the food ranges from grilled chicken to steak, prime rib, roast duck, whitefish, perch, and salmon. It's casual dining, but with tablecloths. There are appetizers and a decent wine list. They offer free shuttle service from the marinas. Prices from $13–25.

Donegal Danny's Pub (231-448-3000), 26420 Carlisle Rd. Open daily, year-round. A friendly Irish bar with pub food and beer on tap. There is seating outdoors. Prices from $8–10.

Shamrock Restaurant & Pub (231-449-2278), 26245 Main St. This place bills itself as the oldest pub on the island. They serve traditional pub fare, but dinners are available. Whitefish, pork, chicken, and steak are the mainstays. Prices from $13–19.

IN EAST JORDAN (JORDAN RIVER, ANTRIM COUNTY CHAIN OF LAKES)

Jordan Inn (231-536-9906; www.jordaninn.com), 288 Main St., East Jordan. This historic inn has a restaurant. Breakfasts of omelets, crepe-style pancakes, and lighter items are available to the public as well as inn guests. Lunch includes salads, soups, and sandwiches. For dinner, there are three- to five-course meals, which include seared duck breasts with pink peppercorn sauce and poached salmon. Prices from $15–25.

Lumber Jack Grill (231-536-2191; www.lumberjackgrill.com), 101 Main St., East Jordan. Open daily. This family-style pub has been a local favorite for years, and serves breakfast, lunch, and dinner. Fare ranges from burgers to prime rib, and of course there's the almost-required fish fry on Friday. They do serve more healthy food in the form of wraps. Prices from $6–15.

Murry's Bar & Grill (231-536-3395; www.murrysbar.com), 115 Main St., East Jordan. Open daily spring and summer. Located near the marina, this family-style pub has a deck overlooking Lake Charlevoix. Burgers are the mainstay here, but there are some surprises, like a pierogi (a potato and cheese appetizer). Prices from $16–18.

IN CENTRAL LAKE (JORDAN RIVER, ANTRIM COUNTY CHAIN OF LAKES)

Blue Pelican Inn & Restaurant (231-544-2583), 2535 North Main St., Central Lake. The menu at this historic inn ranges from seafood to pasta, and has a bit of southern BBQ tossed in. There's an eclectic mix of crab dishes with local perch and walleye. Prices from $20–34.

IN ELLSWORTH (ANTRIM COUNTY CHAIN OF LAKES)

The Rowe Inn (231-588-2365; www.roweinn.com), 6303 CR 48, Ellsworth. Open daily for lunch and dinner. From its rural location, this place has gained a statewide reputation since it opened in 1972, and it has one of the largest wine lists in the state. The menu changes, but its mainstays are beef, veal, lake fish, duck, and lamb. Dining is casual. Reservations are usually needed. Prices from $20–39.

IN FRANKFORT (LAKE MICHIGAN, PLATTE RIVER)

Bunty & JoJo's Casual Restaurant and Tantelle Fine Dining (231-352-7251; www.betsiebayinn.com), 231 Main St., Frankfort. The inn has most of the bases covered when it comes to eating out. They offer casual dining, fine dining, a wine cellar, and a pub all in one building. I'd pick the casual dining, with its reasonable prices yet interesting menu. The salmon cutlet with chorizo sausage, roasted corn, and red pepper sauce is an interesting take on a regional favorite. The whitefish with the roasted red pepper remoulade is another innovative dish. The appetizers in the upscale dining room are items not often found Up North—sautéed potato gnocchi and gratin of wild mushrooms. The Hotspur Pub is decorated like a classic British pub and invites you to spend the evening at one of its round tables. The Thisle Brae Wine Cellar is an intimate place to share a glass of wine with a friend. Prices from $14–25.

IN GLEN ARBOR (LAKE MICHIGAN, PLATTE RIVER)

Good Harbor Grill (231-334-3555), 6584 Western Ave., Glen Arbor. Open daily from May through October for breakfast, lunch, and dinner. Seafood is on the top of the menu, along with steak, chicken, and ribs. There are also vegetarian entrees. Prices from $5–20.

Art's Tavern (231-334-3754; www.artsglenarbor.com), 6487 Western Ave., Glen Arbor. Open daily for breakfast, lunch, and dinner. The fried smelt were a real find. They have been dropped from the menu of many Up North taverns because of their scarcity. The classic "old school" tavern menu pushes up a bit from the usual burgers to charbroiled steaks and fish. Prices from $10–18.

Boone Dock's (231-334-6444), 5858 Manitou (US 22), Glen Arbor. Open daily for lunch and dinner. The log lodge has a large deck that's usually filled with diners. There are burgers, shrimp, and steaks at this sprawling place. Prices from $10–15.

IN LUDINGTON (NORDHOUSE DUNES/LUDINGTON STATE PARK)

PM Steamers (231-843-9555; www.pmsteamers), 502 Ludington Ave., Ludington. This dockside restaurant caters to boaters, with a reliance on steak, seafood, whitefish, and perch. The dishes aren't fancy, but they're designed to please hungry paddlers who have spent a day on the water. Prices from $14–24.

Old Hamlin Restaurant (231-843-4251), 122 W. Ludington Ave., Ludington. This place has been owned and operated by the same family for more than 60 years, and summer visitors and locals keep coming back for the buffet dinners and entrees. Breakfast is served all day, and there's a salad bar and a regular bar. Prices are $8–15.

Luciano's Ristoranti (231-843-2244; www.lucianosristoranti.com), 103 W. Ludington Ave., Ludington. This is the place to go for Italian food in Ludington. The food is top notch, and it's served in an intimate, casual setting. There are pasta dishes, pizza, and panini-style sand-wiches (my favorite is the goat cheese and roasted peppers). There's a good selection of wines. Prices from $10–17.

IN TRAVERSE CITY (GRAND TRAVERSE BAY, SLEEPING BEAR DUNES, PLATTE RIVER, BOARDMAN RIVER)

Bowers Harbor Inn (231-223-4222; www.bowersharborinn.net), 13512 Peninsula Dr., Traverse City. Open daily for dinner. The menu is small, but the choices are excellent at this inn, which was built by a lumber baron. The rack of lamb is done with a pistachio crust, bread pudding, and mint. There are similar treatments for rainbow trout, beef, pork shoulder, and chicken. Try the cheesecake tart for dessert. Prices from $22–34.

Freshwater Lodge Restaurant (231-932-4694; www.michigan menu.com), 13890 S. West Bayshore Dr., Traverse City. Open for lunch and dinner. When it comes to offering a diversified menu, this is the place. Many northern Michigan restaurants have a standard menu with a focus on steaks and whitefish, but the lodge offers much more—and has a few surprises. The steaks are large, and they do have a different twist on the whitefish—a parmesan whitefish. Ribs and chicken are also on the menu. The décor is classic Up North, with a woodsy lodge feeling. The service is excellent. Prices from $14–20.

Mackinaw Brewing Company (231-933-1100), 161 E. Front St., Traverse City. Open for lunch and dinner. This brewpub in the heart of downtown serves up everything from burgers to fine dinners in a historic building. You'll find a lot of locals eating here, and for good reason. The herb-crusted whitefish is a good spin on a traditional northern Michigan dish. A pan-fried walleye with cherries is another favorite—and the burgers are big. The pub brews up its own beers and ales, all of which are worth trying. Prices from $11–17.

North Peak Brewing Company (231-941-7325), 400 W. Front St., Traverse City. The handcrafted beer flows in this restored candy factory. It is a crowded, noisy place that's more of a pub than a restaurant, but there is pizza, steaks, pasta, and sandwiches. Prices from $5–9.

IN MANISTEE (MANISTEE RIVER, LITTLE MANISTEE RIVER, NORDHOUSE DUNES)

The Bungalow Inn (231-723-8000; www.thebungalowinn.com), 1100 28th St., Manistee. Open daily, this is the best full-service restaurant in the community, serving breakfast, lunch, and dinner. There are daily specials and ribs, fish, stir fry, and prime rib—as well as a bar. Prices from $8–21.

House of Flavors (231-887-4600), corner of River Street and US 31, Manistee. This is the place for a paddler to start the day with a hardy breakfast. You'll find many locals here for breakfast, lunch, and dinner. The ice cream is locally made. Prices from $8–10.

River Street Station (231-723-8411), 350 River St., Manistee. This old-style northern Michigan tavern caters to locals and tourists mostly with pub food—but at times it's more ambitious, with homemade soups and prime rib. Prices from $8–12.

IN BALDWIN (PERE MARQUETTE RIVER)

Edie's Log Cabin Bar, MI 37, Baldwin. A great stop for paddlers—it's where locals, anglers, outdoors folks, and fly-fishing guides gather at night for pub food, beer, and conversations. It's good to avoid karaoke night, if you don't like loud music. Prices from $5–10.

IN MACKINAW CITY (WILDERNESS STATE PARK, LAKE MICHIGAN)

There is no shortage of restaurants and fast-food places. Here are a few of the best.

Audie's Restaurant (231-436-5744; www.audies.com), 314 Nicolet St., Mackinaw City. Open daily, year-round. This has been one of my favorite haunts ever since I stopped there with a companion near closing time one January evening—they kept the kitchen open for us. Since it's open year-round, it's a gathering spot for locals. Even though the kitchen staff had to stay late for us, they did a superb job of cooking and serving our meals. There are two restaurants here—a family room with moderately priced meals and the Chippewa Room, which features more upscale meals and a bar. They also serve breakfast. Prices from $18–35.

Dixie Saloon (231-436-5449; www.dixiesaloon.com), 401 E. Central Ave., Mackinaw City. This is the place you want to head to after a long day of paddling. The historic saloon has its origins in the 1890s and was the traditional stopping spot at the end of Old Dixie Highway, a federal road that ran from Florida to Mackinaw City. The log building has an Up North feeling. The ribs are a top attraction. Prices from $15–22.

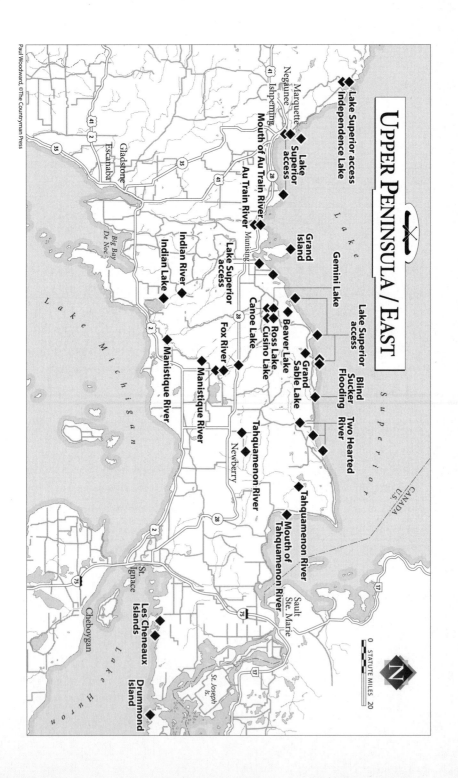

UPPER PENINSULA / EAST

N
STATUTE MILES
0   20

Paul Woodward, ©The Countryman Press

Lake Superior access
Independence Lake

Marquette
Negaunee
Ishpeming

Lake
Superior
access

Mouth of Au Train River
Au Train River

Gladstone
Escanaba

Munising

Big Bay
De Noc

Indian River
Indian Lake

Lake Superior
access

Grand
Island

Gemini Lake

Canoe Lake

Fox River

Beaver Lake
Ross Lake
Cusino Lake

Lake Superior
access

Grand
Sable Lake

Blind
Sucker
Flooding

Two Hearted
River

Manistique River

Manistique River

Newberry

Tahquamenon River

Tahquamenon River
Mouth of
Tahquamenon River

St.
Ignace

Les Cheneaux
Islands

Drummond
Island

Cheboygan

St. Joseph
Is.

Sault
Ste. Marie

CANADA
U.S.

Lake   Superior

Lake   Michigan

Lake   Huron

Part 4 — Eastern Upper Peninsula

Les Cheneaux Islands, Drummond Island, Tahquamenon River, Two-Hearted River, Pictured Rocks National Lakeshore, Grand Island, Hiawatha Water Trail, Fox/Manistique Rivers, Indian River, Au Train River

THIS REGION OFFERS diverse paddling—from the chilly waters of Lake Superior to the warmer ones of Lake Michigan, and in between are rivers and inland lakes. The landscape is low and often brushy, but there are pines and hardwoods—making it a good fall destination to see the colors change.

Apart from St. Ignace, Sault Saint Marie, and Newberry, lodging is mostly found in mom-and-pop-type resorts and motels. There are few chain restaurants, so make sure to pack a lunch when traveling—or go native and pick up some pasties at the various shops on US 2 just west of St. Ignace. Pasties are a UP specialty. The meat, potatoes, and other vegetables wrapped in pastry and baked were brought to the region by Cornish miners in the 19th century, and are a favorite of local residents. They make a great paddling lunch.

The region offers good camping spots, many of them on the water. There are several National Forest campgrounds along US 2 near Epoufette Bay on Lake Michigan. The waters here are warmer than Lake Superior and paddlers could spend several days enjoying shoreline trips.

If you're not into camping, staying at a small resort is a good option. Many offer kitchens, which is a plus in a region which doesn't have a lot of restaurants.

A paddler finds a calm inlet on Lake Superior

The weather here can be iffy. I've seen snow in the middle of May, and large chunks of ice in Lake Superior at that time of year as well. Also, beware of late June because of the black flies, especially along the beaches. They can be nasty. If you make the trip, I'd suggest waiting until early June. Skip late June due to the black flies, and then head out after July Fourth. If you can make it in September, go. The days are cooler, the water is at its warmest point of the summer, and the fall foliage comes early to this part of the country.

Early October can offer some good paddling weather, but early northerly winds can produce some rough water, especially on Lake Superior. By mid-October, I'd stick to the calmer, warmer waters of Lake Michigan, inland lakes, and rivers. By early November, the weather is sketchy, but you may find a few days when you can get out on the water.

Most of the region was logged in the 19th century and much of the land went back to state ownership when the lumberjacks left. This is a real plus for paddlers, because the waters are very accessible. Basically, unless it's posted, most lands are open to the public.

32. Les Cheneaux Islands

Best Runs: 75-mile Northern Lake Huron Paddle Trail, Carp River to
   DeTour
Accessibility: Moderate (most of the islands are privately owned,
   except for Government Island). There are boat launches in
   Cedarville and Hessel, and most lakefront resorts offer access.
Skill Level: Beginner for some spots, but expert for travel among
   the islands
Best Times: May to Oct.
Description: The water is crystal clear, and the beaches sandy
Home Base: Cedarville, Hessel
Location: Eastern UP (east of the Mackinac Bridge), about 20
   miles east of I-75 on MI 134, northern Lake Huron

THIS IS THE PLACE to start if you want to learn sea kayaking. The waters
are generally warm and the islands protect paddlers from the high
waves of northern Lake Huron. The water temperatures can vary depending on wind conditions, so check before going out.

The local outfitter, Woods & Water Ecotours, doesn't rent kayaks—
but it does offer classes and half- or full-day guided tours of the islands.

Paddlers explore the islands

I'd suggest a sea kayak lesson with the guides. They teach paddling skills—but more importantly, rescue techniques. Learning how to self-rescue makes you a much more confidant paddler.

The paddling here can run from a casual evening ride along the Lake Huron shoreline to extended trips along the 75-mile Northern Lake Huron Paddle Trail or trips through the 36 Les Cheneaux Islands.

For beginner and intermediate paddlers, I suggest trying tours along the shoreline either out of Hessel or Cedarville, both of which have public boat launches. A small river kayak or canoe would be fine to use on a calm day along the shoreline, but sea kayaks would be the best choice for travel among the islands.

While there is plenty of water to paddle, there is a shortage of public lands. Government Island is the only island accessible to the public; the others are all private property. Also, much of the Lake Huron shoreline is privately owned.

The islands have a boating heritage dating back to the fur trade era in the 16th and 17th centuries when fur trappers used the islands to get to Mackinac Island, where they traded their furs for goods and money. In the late 19th and early 20th centuries, the islands became home to

Examining an old pier from the islands' past

resort visitors, many of whom arrived by steamships from Chicago, Detroit, and Cleveland.

Travel to and from the resort homes is still done via boat, and Hessel has become a hotspot for wooden boat enthusiasts from around the nation. The town holds its annual Antique Wooden Boat Show and Festival of the Arts in early August, and the event attracts as many as two hundred restored wooden watercraft.

The wooden boat show is the second Saturday in August, and is a good weekend to avoid as it attracts many powerboaters, and the waters can get crowded.

Outfitters

Woods & Water Ecotours (906-484-4157; www.woodswaterecotours .com), 20 Pickford Rd., Hessel. Owner Jessie Hadley has a gem of an enterprise here offering kayak lessons, tours, and extended trips to the islands, nearby Drummond Island, and to Isle Royale in Lake Superior. There are also all-woman tours offered. Rates range from $65 for a two-hour lesson to $125 for a full day of paddling. Extended trips range from $550–750.

33. Drummond Island

Best Runs: Trip to Harbor Island National Wildlife Refuge

Accessibility: Good, about 70 percent of the shoreline is public land and you can launch just about anywhere

Skill Level: Beginner to advanced

Best Times: May to Oct.

Description: The water is crystal clear (look for limestone escarpments)

Home Base: Drummond Island

Location: Eastern UP, about 30 miles east of the Mackinac Bridge, off I-75 on MI 134 on northern Lake Huron, take ferry (has fee) to island

THE FIRST EUROPEANS to visit this island were paddlers, voyageurs from Canada who were loyal to the British and settled portions of the island—

A Half-day Tour of the Islands . . .

We started our 10-mile tour at a boat launch at the end of Lakeside Road just east of Cedarville, and four of us launched our sea kayaks into calm, warm waters for a half-day paddle to Government Island and back.

Our guide said the water was calm enough, so that most any kayak would be adequate, but I was glad to be in the 18-foot sea kayak I'd learned how to manage the previous day, especially the self-rescue technique. Getting yourself back into a boat makes you much more confident about your paddling.

Our paddle took us past the private homes and extensive boat docks that line the shores of most the islands, many dating to the early 20th century when owners of resorts arrived via steamship from places like Detroit, Chicago, and Cleveland.

The landscape is half water and half land—you could easily get lost in the maze of channels unless you had a guide or a good map and knew how to use it. A GPS system would be valuable here, because the land is low, and there are few landmarks.

We followed the Lake Huron lakeshore through Moscoe Channel, into a freshwater marsh, and under a bridge to Hill Island, the only one that's connected to the mainland. We rounded a point of land and Cedarville came into view, looking more like a New England sea coast town than one in Michigan.

We then turned southward between LaSalle Island and Island Number 8, which local legend has it was a typo made by a mapmaker that became permanent. It was a long paddle from there to Government Island, which is open to the public, and I needed a bathroom break. Since the shorelines are in private hands, I had to wait

held by the British until 1828, when it was turned over to America, making it the last disputed piece of land between the two countries.

Settlers eventually made their way to the island, the largest of the more than 900 in the Great Lakes.

While the voyageurs came in their canoes, following the fur trade, these days it's a destination for paddlers, anglers, and hunters attracted by the large parcels of public land (more than 80 percent of the island).

until arriving at Government Island; I made a mental note to add an empty water bottle to my paddling gear for just such emergencies.

By the time we arrived on Government Island, we'd been in our boats for more than two hours; it felt good to get out and stretch my legs. The island is laced with formal and informal campgrounds, and we hiked across the island with our lunches and found a good spot with a picnic table on Lake Huron. In just that short walk, we went from the calm island waters to the rougher waters of the open lake.

Our afternoon paddle took us to Boot Island, where we could look out and see the open waters, and around Coryell Island, and then back to the boat launch. The trip gave us a good feeling for the islands, their historic homes, their boat houses, and the camping grounds on Government Island.

Touring the Les Cheneaux islands

For paddlers that translates into an infinite number of possibilities. The ultimate trip is the 75-mile trek around the island, camping as you go. The trip takes four or five days and is for those with advanced kayaking skills. The trip involves long paddles and the ability to do wilderness camping on undeveloped state land.

For those looking for day trips, Potagannissing Bay is the best destination. For beginner and intermediate paddlers, a trip along the shoreline from the Township Park Campground boat launch is a good introduction to the island. The bay is fairly well sheltered from the north winds by the many outer islands.

For those with better skills, a prime destination is Harbor Island Wildlife Refuge. Though public land, there's no camping allowed. Camping is allowed on Bow Island, which is about 3 miles northwest of the Township Park Campground and 1 mile north of Sims Point on the mainland. Most of the islands are privately owned, and have summer homes located on them.

If you really want a remote area, head to Glen Cove on the island's eastern shore. It's accessible via Glen Cove Road, but make sure you're driving a sturdy, four-wheel-drive vehicle as the road isn't much more than a snowmobile trail at some points. Launch at Glen Cove and head either north or south along the shoreline, which is part of the Heritage Water Trail. This would also be a good place to launch from if you're planning to circumnavigate the island.

34. Tahquamenon River

Best Runs: Dollarville to Lake Superior, 65 miles, 4–6 days
Accessibility: Fair
Skill Level: Beginner to intermediate
Best Times: May to Oct.
Description: Fairly slow-moving, dark, deep tea-colored water
Home Base: Paradise, Newberry
Location: Eastern UP, off MI 28 via MI 123

TAHQUAMENON FALLS are a top tourist attraction and offer visitors a chance to see two of the larger falls east of the Mississippi. The 200-foot-wide by 50-foot-high upper falls, and 23-foot-high lower falls, are in the 45,000-acre Tahquamenon Falls State Park and attract about half a million people annually.

The first historical mention of the falls came from Henry Wadsworth Longfellow in his poem Song of Hiawatha, a pretty good exercise in creative writing since Longfellow never set foot in Michigan.

The park, which has some virgin timber, has 40 miles of hiking

A boat pulled up on a northern Michigan riverbank

trails, 20,000 acres of natural areas, 13 inland lakes, and an interpretative nature center. There are moose, wolves, bear, and 125 species of birds in the park.

Both Newberry and Paradise offer accommodations and restaurants, most of which are either family-style places or taverns. More options are to be found in Newberry. While in the area, a side trip to Whitefish Point is rewarding, with birdwatching and a nautical museum as attractions.

Dollarville Dam to Sixteen Creek State Forest Campground (9 miles, 2–3 hours): Quick waters, tight turns

An easy day paddle for beginners, with waters 40–50 feet wide making for easy paddling. The waters move fairly fast, but slow near Spider Bay, a marshy area. Get out at the campground—the next take-out point is 30 miles downstream.

Sixteen Creek State Forest Campground to Upper Tahquamenon Falls (30 miles, 8–10 hours): Private property, anglers, and a portage

This is a long, hard slog that should be planned out ahead of time, and should be done by experienced expedition paddlers. Not only do you have 30 miles to cover in a day, but also a portage at the end of the trip—and then the need to find a camping place, if you're doing multiple days on the river. To lighten the load and make it easy at day's end, set up a camp at the state park the previous day and paddle to it the next. There is some public land along the river, but much of it is low and marshy and not good for camping. The river is nearly 100 feet wide and deep as it passes through lowlands on this run, and it is fairly heavily fished by motorboats.

Paddlers will be warned by signs about the upcoming waterfalls when entering the state park, but stay alert; this is coming at the end of a long paddling day.

Upper Tahquamenon Falls to Lake Superior (19 miles, 6–8 hours): Another portage, a remote wilderness area

The day starts with another portage around the lower falls, and then it's an easy 15-mile trip through a remote area with no access points until reaching Lake Superior 5 miles south of Paradise. The river broadens to 100–150 feet and the landscape is sandy and piney, with marsh areas.

Outfitters

Tahquamenon General Store (906-492-3560; www.exploringthenorth
.com/tahquagen/store), 39991 W. MI 123, Paradise. The store offers canoe/kayak rentals for 17-mile trips on the river from the Lower Falls to the river mouth at Whitefish Bay, and rental boats for use on local inland lakes. They also offer shuttle service those who own their own boats. The shuttle cost is $25.

The Woods, Tahquamenon River Canoe & Kayak Rental (906-203-7624; www.thewoodscanoerental.net), corner of MI 123 and Fordney Tower Rd., 13 miles north of Newberry. Open daily from mid-June through mid-September. No credit cards. The livery offers trips on the upper portion of the river above the falls. It also offers shuttle service for those with their own boats.

35. Two-Hearted River

Best Runs: Reed and Green Bridge to Lake Superior
Accessibility: Fair
Skill Level: Beginner to intermediate
Best Times: Mid-May to early Oct.
Description: Tea-colored water, fairly wide, some fallen logs
Home Base: Rainbow Lodge, mouth of river
Location: Eastern UP, 34 miles north of Newberry off County Road H37 (CR H37)

THIS RIVER HAS a great name, so good that Ernest Hemingway borrowed it for a well-known short story, even though the river he was writing about was actually the Fox—far to the west, near Seney.

It's a problematic river to paddle because there are only two access points, and it can be bug intensive—especially in late June during the black fly season. There are also many fallen logs in the river from the High Bridge access point to Reed and Green Bridge. The river can be fast, and quick maneuvering skills are needed to avoid tipping-over experiences.

I'd save this trip for late August through early October, when there are fewer bugs. It's a great fall destination for a color tour.

High Bridge to Reed and Green Bridge (9 miles, 6–9 hours):
Fallen trees to portage over

I really can't recommend this section of the river to recreational paddlers. I took this trip one fall, and it was a long, wet trudge by the end of the day. I tipped over several times, and had to lift my canoe over fallen logs countless times. Many of the fallen logs are located in bends of the river, which are difficult to negotiate anyway. My time estimate could be a lot longer, depending on a paddler's skills.

Reed and Green Bridge to Lake Superior (11 miles, 4–5 hours):
Better recreational paddling

This stretch is much easier, although there can be some obstructions. The river is up to 50 feet wide here and 2–4 feet deep, and downed trees can be gotten around much easier. The tea-colored water moves quickly and good reactions are still needed, but much of it can simply be floated. I like floating it in the fall during the annual steelhead run. It's fun to watch the big lunkers moving through the water. The high, sandy banks are mostly covered with pines and birch, but with occasional sand dunes. The river's mouth comes just after passing under a swinging bridge. During the fall, paddlers will encounter anglers in wooden drift boats. The Two-Hearted River Forest Campground at the mouth provides access and parking.

Outfitters

Rainbow Lodge (906-658-3357; www.exploringthenorth.com/two heart/rainbow), 32752 CR 423, Newberry. The lodge and canoe livery is located at the mouth of the Two-Hearted River on Lake Superior, and is really the only place around. It offers lodging, a campground, and a general store catering to outdoors people. They offer car spotting services for those with their own boats.

36. Pictured Rocks National Lakeshore

Best Runs: Munising to Grand Marais, 40 miles, 4–6 days
Accessibility: Fair
Skill Level: Intermediate to advanced for trips along Pictured Rocks, beginner for day trips from Grand Marais
Best Times: Mid-May to Sept.
Description: The waters of Lake Superior are quite cold, but you'll find warmer waters in the Grand Marais Harbor
Home Base: Munising, Grand Marais
Location: Central UP, north of MI 28

THE GREAT LAKES Kayak Symposium, one of the largest in the Midwest, is held in Grand Marais in mid-July for good reason—the area offers diverse paddling, from the calm, warm waters of Grand Marais Harbor for beginners to the cold waters of Lake Superior along the Pictured Rocks for those with advanced skills. There are also numerous inland lakes that offer quiet waters, and several nearby rivers that can be floated.

The top trip here would be a paddle from Munising to Grand Marais, along the Pictured Rocks National Lakeshore, heading from west to east and working with the prevailing westerly winds, which would make the trip easier.

The lakeshore, administered by the National Park Service, has about 40 miles of Lake Superior shoreline and campsites along the way for backpackers, but which are easily accessed by paddlers. If you're going to do the entire trip, I'd suggest you schedule at least five days—you're going to do a lot of exploring on shore and sightseeing, especially along the Pictured Rocks, which rise 50–200 feet above Lake Superior.

While much of the waters are rated for beginner or intermediate skills, it would be good to have one person in your party with advanced skills if you choose to negotiate paddling along the 15-mile Pictured Rocks shoreline. Paddlers should have self-rescue skills because much of the coast doesn't have a shoreline, and is pure rock. Weather can also be a factor. Check the forecast first.

Going with a kayak guide on a tour of the Pictured Rocks is a good

Kayakers explore the cliffs along Lake Superior

A rough day on Lake Superior's cold waters

option, especially for beginner and even intermediate paddlers. That way you have an expert with you (see *Outfitters*). For intermediate paddlers, a day with a guide will help you become accustomed to the area; from there, you could plan your own trips without the guide.

Those venturing into Lake Superior should at the very least wear a wet suit. The water rarely gets above 50 degrees—with one, you can survive being in the water for four hours.

Weather and Waters

The U.S. Coast Guard classifies the Great Lakes as arctic waters, and that's probably not much of a surprise to those who know Lake Superior. The average year-round temperature is 40 degrees, though it does warm in the summer—but not enough to swim comfortably in the open lake. If you're planning a trip, especially in the early spring or fall, check the weather conditions before you go. There have been chucks of ice floating in the lake as late as mid-May. While October can be a gentle month in Lake Huron and Lake Michigan, Superior is susceptible to storms from the north.

Lake waves are choppier than ones on the ocean, giving paddlers less time to recover between waves. Times of day are important, too; early morning and early evening hours often offer some of the calmest paddling of the day.

Day Trips

Here are some day trips for those who aren't going to make the long trek from Munising to Grand Marais. Check with the Park Service before planning a trip.

Dunes Trip: You won't see the Pictured Rocks on this trip, but you will be able to see the impressive dunes. It's about a 10-mile trip to the Hurricane River, at which there's a campground and a good take-out spot for boats. For a long but rewarding day trip, put in at the Hurricane River and paddle to Grand Marais. For expert paddlers, this is about a 4-hour trip, but there are plenty of places to stop and admire the dunes, so it could easily be a 6–7 hour trip. Sable Falls near Grand Marais would be a welcome stop and a rewarding walk. The breakwater at the mouth of Grand Marais Harbor presents some difficult paddling, with complex currents. This can be avoided by beaching your boat at Woodland Park, the township campgrounds along the beach, or the beach just before the breakwall. There's a small gravel parking lot there that requires no permit or parking fee.

Sand Point to Miner's Castle: Located 4 miles east of Munising off of CR H58, Sand Point is a good place to launch for a day trip along the Pictured Rocks or to make the crossing over to Grand Island, which offers similar cliff views. There's a boat launch at Sand Point, but you can also launch from the parking lot as it's only about 30 yards to the water. Even on days with high waves, Grand Island offers a good buffer from the winds until you get to the start of the Pictured Rocks. Paddlers could spend most of a day here exploring the lakeshore. A good destination would be Miner's Beach—a sandy, mile-long beach just east of Miner's Castle.

Miner's Beach: Launching from the beach puts a paddler in the middle of the Pictured Rocks, but it comes at a price. The beach is about 100 yards from the parking lot, and that includes about 50 sets of stairs. The reward is almost limitless paddling along the Pictured Rocks. Paddlers could spend a day or several days paddling from this access point.

Beaver Lake: This paddle offers the possibility of either a day or several day paddles that include travel on an inland lake and Lake Superior. Located off of CR H58, the launch is at Beaver Lake Campgrounds, and the trip takes paddlers through Little and Big Beaver lakes and into Lake Superior via Beaver Creek. The creek is too shallow to paddle, so travelers are required to get out of their boats and pull them while wading to Lake Superior, about 0.25 mile north. Having a rope is a good idea.

A creek running from Beaver Lake to Lake Superior

The creek is on the north side of Beaver Lake and is so small that it can be easily missed. There are three campsites on Lake Superior near the mouth of Beaver Creek—Coves (to the west) and Beaver Creek and Pine Bluff to the east. The Pictured Rocks are about 2 miles to the west.

Inland Lakes

But while the big lake is the top attraction, other smaller inland lakes and flooding areas make for interesting trips—especially for those who don't have high degrees of kayak skills. On the top of my list is Grand Sable Lake near Grand Marais. The National Park Service, which administers the lakeshore, main-

The Grand Sable Dunes loom over the lake

tains a boat launch on the lake—but it's very difficult for motorboats to launch, and while you'll see a few anglers on occasion, the lake is pretty much a haven for paddlers. It offers a great view of the dunes and wildlife, including beaver and eagles. A trip around the lake takes about two hours if you follow the shoreline.

Little Beaver Lake is also a great destination. Located 3 miles north of CR H58, the lake offers a secluded campground with about a dozen campsites and a boat launch. There are actually two lakes here, Little Beaver and Beaver. A small creek runs out of the north end of the larger lake and into Lake Superior, giving paddlers access to the Pictured Rocks. The creek can't actually be paddled, but a paddler can easily pull a boat along it while walking the bank. It's a great location from which to take a day trip to the Pictured Rocks, which start just west of the Beaver Lakes area.

Blind Sucker Flooding

The name sounds unappealing, but the paddling isn't. Located off CR H58, about 5 miles east of Grand Marais, the flooding area is accessed via the Blind Sucker Campground just north of the main road. At first sight, it appears as through you're launching in a landscape of half land, half water—but don't let that deter you. Paddlers can wander it for an entire day. The pike fishing is legendary. Follow the water trails through the tall grasses and look for heron and other wildlife. If you have a GPS unit, this is a good place to use it. A map isn't of much help. I've paddled it often in a canoe and have never gotten truly lost, but I try keeping general track of which direction I'm traveling with a compass. Paddlers can spend a few hours or an entire day here. For families, a paddling/camping trip here would be a good way to introduce children to both. The waters are calm and not deep. One warning—the black flies can be vicious in late June and can ruin a trip. I'd plan it for mid-July through August.

Gemini, Ross, Cusino, and Canoe Lakes

If you're paddling the Pictured Rocks and the weather puts you off the water, the four inland lakes south of the Pictured Rocks National

Lakeshore make a good destination and a possible camping spot from which to explore the area.

While the federal campgrounds on the Lake Superior lakeshore can get crowded during summer months, the five state campgrounds on the inland lakes are rarely filled. There is a daily camping fee.

Gemini and Ross are the most interesting to paddle, with intricate shorelines and islands on Ross Lake to explore. You could spend an entire day on each lake. Perch fishing is particularly good.

Directions: The lakes and campgrounds are in remote backwoods locations, but there are good gravel roads leading to them with sign postings. A good route is off MI 77, between Grand Marais and Seney, on Adams Trail (which runs to Munising). The lakes are slightly more than 12 miles off MI 77 on Adams Trail. Turn left (south) on Crooked Lake Road for Ross Lake, and left (south) for Gemini Lake. From the Munising area, take CR H58 for about 17 miles to the lake area. The area is in Schoolcraft County, and the roads there can be confusing, so make sure to have a set of county maps (the Michigan Atlas and Gazetteer from DeLorme are the best).

Outfitters

Woods & Water Ecotours (906-484-4157; www.woodswaterecotours .com), 20 Pickford Rd., Hessel. Owner Jessie Hadley offers tours to the Pictured Rocks—as well as to Les Cheneaux Islands, nearby Drummond Island, and to Isle Royale in Lake Superior. There are also all-woman tours offered. Rates range from $65 for a two-hour lesson to $125 for a full day of paddling. Extended trips range from $550–750.

Resources

Pictured Rocks National Lakeshore (906-387-2607; www.nps.gov /piro/index.htm), Headquarters, N8391 Sand Point Rd., Munising; Grand Sable Visitors Center, about 2 miles west of Grand Marais on CR H58. Open summer only. Those taking extended trips along the Lake Superior shoreline through the Pictured Rocks are required to obtain permits from the National Park Service, which are available at either office. The Park Service's Web site provides good maps and information about kayaking and camping.

37. Grand Island

Best Runs: 27-mile circumnavigation of the island (extended trip), day trips around Murray Bay and Mather Beach area
Accessibility: Good
Skill Level: Intermediate to advanced (beginners, if with an outfitter)
Best Times: Mid-May to Sept.
Description: Lake Superior waters are clear and cold, about 40–50 degrees in the summer
Home Base: Munising
Location: Central UP, north of MI 28

YOU COULD SPEND a week paddling here without exhausting the possibilities. While a trip around the island is the ultimate paddle, there are other day trips that aren't as arduous. The northern two-thirds of the island has cliffs 50–400 feet high with no landing places for paddlers. Also, the island is exposed to the rough waves of Lake Superior and water temperatures that barely hit 50 degrees during the summer. There's also the 0.5-mile paddle to the island from the mainland to contend with.

If you're going to try going around the island, it would be a good idea to have at least one advanced paddler in your group. I wouldn't suggest that two intermediate paddlers try the trip. Anyway, there are plenty of possibilities on the south end of the island.

A good Grand Island sampler paddle would be from William's Landing, where the visitor contact station is located along the shoreline of Murray Bay, to the Murray Bay group campsites. Set up camp here, and the next day head to either Flat Rock or Cobble Cove campground, both of which are accessible from the water. The trip takes paddlers along the cliffs. From Cobble Cove, paddlers could spend a day exploring Trout Bay, which is sheltered from Lake Superior.

The best paddling access point for kayakers is from Sand Point, about

4 miles east of Munising on CR H58. It's about a 0.5-mile paddle to the island, and the waters are protected from the open lake waves by the island.

Outfitters

Woods & Water Ecotours (906-484-4157, www.woodswaterecotours .com), 20 Pickford Rd., Hessel. Owner Jessie Hadley offers tours to the Pictured Rocks, as well as to Les Cheneaux Islands, nearby Drummond Island, and to Isle Royale in Lake Superior. There are also all-woman tours offered. Rates range from $65 for a two-hour lesson to $125 for a full day of paddling. Extended trips range from $550–750.

38. Hiawatha Water Trail

Best Runs: Big Bay to Grand Marais, 120 miles, 10–15 days
Accessibility: Good at various points
Skill Level: Intermediate to advanced
Best Times: Late May to Sept.
Description: Lake Superior waters are clear and cold, about 40–50 degrees in the summer
Home Base: Big Bay, Marquette, Munising, and Grand Marais
Location: Central UP, north of MI 28
Boat Suggestion: Sea kayak with self-rescue gear

THIS SPRAWLING TRAIL is a challenge that some will take up. It can be done by hard-core paddlers accustomed to long paddling days and wilderness camping, but it won't attract most recreational paddlers. The U.S. Park Service recommends that average paddlers try covering no more than 10 miles daily, and 15 miles for experts. That would make it a 15-day trip, in the best of conditions.

The trail does take paddlers along the stunning and rocky Lake Superior shoreline, but much of the route is exposed to

Preparing to launch a canoe

Kayakers load up after a trip

the open (and rough) waters of the big lake. As material for the trail suggests, it should be paddled from Big Bay (northwest of Marquette) to Grand Marais, which is from west to east. That way paddlers take advantage of the prevailing westerly winds.

The trail is marked in some places, with the eastern portion being the most developed where it runs from Munising through the Pictured Rocks National Lakeshore, and work is being done on the portion between Marquette and Munising. The biggest gap is between Big Bay and Little Presque Isle, a 25-mile stretch of private lands where there is no legal shore access.

There's an alternative to doing the entire 120 miles, and that's combining a paddling/driving trip along the shoreline, stopping to paddle the most interesting and accessible places. My suggestion would be to make stops at Big Bay, Marquette, the Laughing Whitefish riverboat ramp, Au Train Beach, and Munising. That would take at least a week (see Grand Island National Recreation Area and Pictured Rocks for that section of the lake).

Big Bay

Nestled near the Huron Mountains, this quirky town is a getaway for folks from Marquette. Take County Road 550 (CR 550) northwest out of Marquette. The ride takes you through a remote area, with views of the Huron Mountains. Launch at Big Bay Harbor for a day tour around it. There's a lighthouse to see, but it's privately owned and operated as a bed & breakfast (see *Lodging*). If the big lake is too rough, check out Independence Lake for paddling. It's off CR 550 in a county park.

Marquette

Paddlers could spend several days here enjoying the sandy beaches, lighthouses, and harbors by day and the upscale lodging and dining opportunities of this college town. Access to Lake Superior is nearly limitless in this city, which has embraced its shoreline; if you tire of paddling, there's a bicycle trail along the shoreline.

With its large population of students at Northern Michigan University, the city has long embraced the outdoor lifestyle, and during warmer months you'll see people out and about in kayaks and on bicycles.

If you're looking for a good workout, this would be the place to bring a bicycle. It would be easy to lock it up some place along your route, paddle to it, and then bike back to your vehicle.

Little Presque Isle to South Beach Park (11 miles, 5–7 hours): Rocky shorelines, islands, lighthouse

Put in at Little Presque Isle off CR 550 via Harlow Lake Road, 5.5 miles northwest of Marquette. It's a short paddle to Little Presque Isle, with pretty but boat-grabbing boulders around it. Head southwest toward Marquette along the exposed rocky shoreline, and pause to look at the sandstone cliffs. When you see Partridge Island, you're about to enter Partridge Bay. Look for Middle Island Point. The lake is more sheltered here by the islands. Paddle through Middle Bay to the 328-acre Presque Isle Park, which is on a peninsula that juts into the big lake. When you paddle around it, you'll see a breakwall that guards Presque Isle Harbor. Watch out for the currents at the end of the wall. There's a take-out on a beach next to the Presque Isle Marina. Watch out for lake freighters coming into the ore docks. Picnic Rocks appear on the left and across from them on the mainland is Shiras Park, a sandy beach that could serve as a good spot for a lunch break, or a take-out point. There's parking along the road, and a short boat carry. On the right is downtown Marquette with its Victorian homes and 19th century sandstone commercial buildings—the Landmark Hotel is the tallest. Look for a red lighthouse on a rocky shore. On the left is McCarty's Cove, another good take-out or launch.

On the right is another breakwall to paddle around—again, watch out for the currents. Entering Marquette Bay is a delight, with the sailboats in the marina and older buildings in the background. The calm harbor makes for a gentle paddle, and it's a good place to pause. The take-out is at South Beach Park, just off Lake Street. It's off US 41 south of Marquette. There's also a take-out spot at the Chocolay River boat ram off MI 28.

Laughing Whitefish Riverboat Launch (15 miles, 3.5 hours): Exposed, rocky shoreline

The put-in is near the mouth of the Laughing Whitefish River, and is accessed off MI 28 via CR 483, about 17 miles west of Marquette. Make a left on North Pointe Road, which leads to the launch—the trip is about 2.5 miles. At several points CR 483 is called Laughing Whitefish Road and North Pointe Road. The water is slow near the mouth, but prepare for the sight of Lake Superior as you paddle out of it. You can encounter some rough seas on this exposed, rocky point. Before driving out here, I usually check the status of the big lake, stopping at one of two rest areas off MI 28 several miles to the west. If the lake isn't too rough you can take your pick and paddle west or east; however, if there are high seas, paddle east around Laughing Whitefish Point where you'll find the more sheltered Au Train Bay. It's a 15-mile paddle to the Au Train boat ramp, a long day for most recreational paddlers.

Au Train Boat Ramp (6 miles, 2.5 hours): Sandy beaches, mouth of Au Train River

This boat ramp is just off MI 28 about 12 miles west of Munising. The waters of the somewhat-protected Au Train Bay can be calm, even on rough days, and the spot can be a trip saver. Just to the west is the rocky Laughing Whitefish Point; to the east, sandy beaches and the mouth of the Au Train River. Try a paddle to the mouth of the Au Train River (and upstream a bit more) for an easy 6-mile round-trip day.

Sand Point Beach: Munising (South Bay), Grand Island, Pictured Rocks

This is a good access point for starting trips that can last for a few hours or for several days. The beach is about 4 miles from downtown Munising on Sand Point Road via MI 28, and gives paddlers many options—including day trips to Grand Island or the Pictured Rocks (see those sections) or around South Bay for a view of the town which is stretched out along MI 28 and hemmed in by large rock escarpments and Lake Superior. The put-in is good for multiple day trips to Grand Island or the Pictured Rocks. There's plenty of parking and a boat launch.

39. Fox/Manistique Rivers

Best Runs: Germfask to Merwin Creek campgrounds, 45 miles, 2–3 days
Accessibility: Fair
Skill Level: Intermediate to advanced (beginners with an outfitter)
Best Times: Mid-May to Sept.
Description: Upper portions choked with fallen trees
Home Base: Germfask
Location: Central UP, MI 77 between US 2 and MI 28

THE RIVER SYSTEM offers paddlers a rugged, backwoods experience on the Fox River from Seney for 15 miles to where it joins the Manistique River, and then a gentle ride on a broad river where you can take your family from there downstream as far as Manistique.

The Fox entices many, including Ernest Hemingway—who based his story "The Big Two-Hearted River" on a fishing trip he took with friends to the Fox near Seney. The story prompted his son, Jack, to try fishing the Two-Hearted River (which is nearby). When he told his author father about the trip, the elder Hemingway told him he'd fished the Fox—but liked the name "Two-Hearted" better.

The access points for the Fox are either at the Seney Township campground, about 2 miles north of MI 28 on the Fox River Road, or further upriver at the State Forest Campground, about 5 miles from Seney.

Unless you're hard-core, I wouldn't suggest paddling any further upriver than the campground. I've fly-fished that part of the river for more than 35 years, and have occasionally seen the most miserable paddlers I've encountered in my life—mosquito-bitten souls, wet up to their necks from pulling their canoes over the numerous downed logs.

If you're looking for a challenge, at least try the section from Seney downriver to Germfask. You'll get wet enough there pulling your boat over downed logs, but at least the river is wider—and folks with chainsaws have hacked some water pathways through the downed logs.

The stretch of river for several miles south of Seney is called "the spreads" because the river splits into a maze of narrow waterways. It has a reputation of being a prime spot for large brook trout—but don't try a fly rod, there's just not enough room for one. You're better off dunking some worms using a short rod.

The trip from Seney to Germfask is supposed to take six to eight hours, but it took much longer when I floated it—partly because I did a lot of fishing, and also because I encountered many downed logs that required me to portage over them.

There were rewards. I saw otter and wildfowl, and heard black bear in the low, brushy areas. Birdwatchers may be attracted to the trip as the river flows through the Seney National Wildlife Refuge.

The trip could easily be turned into a two-day affair, but there are few decent camping spots available—especially during the first 6 miles. After that, there are a few open places—but not a lot, so don't be picky.

Once you arrive at the point where the east branch of the Fox meets the west, the paddling becomes easier. The river widens to 30–40 feet and there are fewer downed trees—I didn't have to go into the water once to pull my boat over one.

Bug Alert!

The black flies and mosquitoes can be miserable in this river system. Late June through early July brings on the black flies, which can be worse than mosquitoes. Many of the insects breed and hatch is the vast Seney National Wildlife Refuge, which is composed of marshland. I've fished and paddled the area for 35 years, and have noticed that there are more bugs when the winds come from the south and west—I suspect it blows them out of the Seney swamps. North winds usually bring relief from the bugs.

Fox River

MI 28 Bridge in Seney to Germfask (16 miles, 7–12 hours): Logs across river, narrow water

This is one of the most exhausting paddles I've ever done in my life, and I wouldn't recommend it as a casual trip, except for hard-core paddlers looking for a challenge. The river starts gently in Seney—40–50 feet wide, and deep enough that you don't scrape bottom, even during the summer. But within 2 miles you hit "the spreads" area, where the river splits apart into channels. Head for the widest ones, and even doing that you'll end up having to turn around and try another occasionally. The trout fishing is very good here, with the deep waters holding trout. If you're going to fish it, plan to camp overnight—you won't get back until long after dark. Good camping sites are rare in the spreads; I only found one on high ground. After leaving the spreads, there's about 10 miles of tough paddling, with countless downed trees across the river. Plan on getting wet, because you're going to have to lift your boat over those logs; I wished I had used one of those small river kayaks for the trip. When you hit the juncture with the East Branch of the Fox, the float becomes more pleasant. The river widens, and there are few logs lying across it. As you near Germfask, you'll see a few homes and cabins—the first of the trip. There's a good take-out at Northland Outfitters and another at a roadside park at the MI 77 Bridge.

Manistique River

This is a good river for introducing a family to canoe camping in a semiwild landscape, with its 67 river miles from Germfask to Manistique on Lake Michigan. There are numerous formal campgrounds and many other informal ones along the river. The trip takes paddlers through portions of the Seney National Wildlife Refuge, and there are opportunities to see wolves, bear, and other wildlife.

Germfask to Mead Creek Campground (12 miles, 4–5 hours): Wide river, wildlife refuge

The best place to put in is at Northland Outfitters, otherwise you're looking at tough access at Ten Curves Road or at the public rest area at the MI 77 Bridge. This stretch can almost be done by drifting and steering, and would be a good trip with kids. There are some fallen logs, but the river is wide enough so you can easily negotiate your way around them. Much of the low hills landscape is part of the Seney National Wildlife Refuge, so watch out for bird life. There's no camping allowed on the refuge. Mead Creek Campground is on the left, and is easily found.

Mead Creek Campground to Merwin Creek Campground (29 miles, 7–9 hours): Easy float

The trip could be made shorter by taking out at Cookson Bridge, which has good access and is only a 12-mile trip. The river is up to 120 feet wide, and the downed trees are easily maneuvered around. It passes through the Manistique River State Forest, and there is little development. I'd suggest ending your trip at Merwin Creek Campground. The river slows for the next 22 miles as it moves toward the city of Manistique, and there are backwaters filled with black flies and mosquitoes.

Attractions

Seney National Wildlife Refuge (906-586-9851; www.fws.gov /midwest/seney), 5 miles south of Seney on MI 77, 2 miles north of Germfask. The refuge is a breeding ground for migratory birds and other wildlife, and is open daily to the public mid-May through mid-October. There are driving tours and ponds where wildlife can be seen.

Outfitters

Northland Outfitters (906-586-9801; www.northoutfitters.com), MI 77, Germfask. Tom Kenney, the owner, is the river master here, offering trips on the Fox and Manistique rivers—and plenty of good advice. There are also cabins and campsites for rent.

40. Indian River

> **Best Runs:** Fish Lake to 8 Mile, 30 miles
> **Accessibility:** Good
> **Skill Level:** Beginner to intermediate
> **Best Times:** Mid-May to Sept.
> **Description:** Classic UP stream, tea-colored water
> **Home Base:** Munising
> **Location:** South of Munising off CR H13

THE INDIAN IS another one of those UP tea-colored rivers known for its trout fishing, but in recent years it has become a paddling destination thanks to the Hiawatha National Forest, which has established a canoe/kayak trail and keeps it maintained by removing fallen logs in some parts of the river.

The river rises out of Doe Lake, but the river isn't maintained for the first 5 miles until it reaches Fish Lake; from there to 8 Mile, the next 30 miles are cleared. The river winds its way through forestland (mostly public) and meadows on its way to Indian Lake. Access is good most of the way, and a variety of trips could be planned—including overnight camping.

There are some gentle paddles where you could take children, but other sections call for advanced skills.

Black bear are numerous, along with deer, beaver, bobcat, coyote—and even wolf. It's a good place to see bald eagles and one of the few places in the state to see sandhill cranes—along with herons, grouse, and woodcock. Trout fishing is good below Delias Run.

Pausing on a river

The river is in a fairly remote area of the UP, and is about 25 miles south of Munising. Few canoe liveries service the river, so plan on bringing your own boat. That may be off-putting to some, but it means there is little traffic on the river.

Fish Lake to Thunder Lake Road (13.2 miles, 6–7 hours): Narrow waters, a portage

Paddlers can also put in at Wide Waters Campground about 1 mile downstream off Forest Road 2262 (FR 2262) off CR H13. The river winds through upland forests and is only 15–30 feet wide. The scattered hardwoods and white birch would make it a colorful fall paddle. Watch for some swift water above the CR H13 Bridge. There's a portage into Straits Lake, and the river flows through Deep and Corner lakes. There's a canoe campsite on this stretch. The river widens to up to 50 feet after hitting the Tommy Page Bridge. Look for Blue Joe Hill, a white birch forest. From McCormick Access to Thunder Lake Road, the river flows through a semiprimitive nonmotorized area, with four campsites. The banks are steep and erosion is serious, so the forest service asks people not to climb them.

Thunder Lake Road to Indian River Campground (9.7 miles, 3–6 hours): Not for novices

Logs in the river can make for a long paddle on this stretch, and some paddlers will have to get out and lift their boats over the logs—or even portage around. There's a take-out at the Indian River Campground, a fee area. There are also two other campsites along this stretch.

Indian River Campground to 8 Mile Bridge (7 miles, 3 hours): Into the spreads

The river moves from high country forestland into marshlands, and the river divides into various channels called "the upper spreads." It's great trout habitat.

8 Mile Bridge to Indian Lake (10 miles, 4–5 hours): For hard-core paddlers

The last section of the river is for those seeking backwoods experiences, as the river enters "the lower spreads," a series of shallow, fingerlike channels. There's no road access, and even when you reach Indian Lake it's another 2 miles of paddling to the boat launch in a state park.

41. Au Train River

Best Runs: Au Train Lake to Lake Superior
Accessibility: Good
Skill Level: Beginner
Best Times: Mid-May to Sept.
Description: Lake Superior waters are clear and cold, about 40–50 degrees in the summer
Home Base: Au Train
Location: Central UP, north of MI 28

THIS IS A GREAT RIVER for introducing children to the joys of paddling, with no portages and a gentle current that moves along to Lake Superior. There are wildlife viewing opportunities and warm-water fishing. The river starts at Au Train Lake and veers to the west, and then back east. Paddlers can pretty much walk back about 0.5 mile to their vehicles.

A relaxed summer day on a river

Au Train is a popular resort destination, with its sandy Lake Superior beach and warm waters from the river flowing into it, making for good swimming. Much of the area is part of the Hiawatha National Forest, and there are several campgrounds in the area. There are also numerous cottages and cabins for rent, many including the use of canoes/kayaks (see *Lodging*).

CR H03 Bridge to Lake Superior (10 miles, 4–6 hours): A short walk back

Put in at the northern bridge where CR H03 crosses the Au Train River, and gently paddle the winding 10 miles to Lake Superior—where, if you take out at MI 28, it's only a short walk back to your vehicle.

In the Area

Lodging

IN HESSEL/CEDARVILLE (LES CHENEAUX ISLANDS)

Hessel Bay Sunset Cabins (906-484-3913; www.hesselsunsetcabins .com), 3347 W. Lake St., Hessel. After a day of paddling there's nothing better than a rustic cabin along the lake that offers a kitchen where you can do your own cooking, a place to hang out, and plenty of room to dry out your gear. This place fits that bill. You could also launch your kayak from here, which would make it a great home base. The six cabins have fully equipped kitchens and appliances, so you can wash those paddling clothes. All the cabins have two bedrooms, each with a double bed. Summer rates $155 daily, $945 weekly.

Les Cheneaux Landing (906-484-2558; www.lclanding.com), 1158 S. Park Ave., Cedarville. This 12-cabin resort is made for large groups with ten units with two bedrooms and two others with four bedrooms, all with full-size beds. The cabins sleep from four to ten people, and have fully equipped kitchens. There are boat launching facilities. Weekly rates from $585–995.

Lake View Motel & Cottages (906-484-2474), 3078 W. Lake Street, Hessel. This is one of the few motels in the area, and it offers single rooms that are both knotty-pine décor and clean—just the thing after a day on the water. The motel has a lakefront location and a boat launch for paddlers. It's easy to find—just look for the lime-green buildings. Rates from $55–100.

ON DRUMMOND ISLAND (LAKE HURON)

Fort Drummond Marine & Resort (906-493-5359; www.fort drummondmarine.com), 36183 S. Whitney Bay Rd. This is a boater's refuge, with five neat and clean housekeeping cabins offering two, three, and four bedrooms. The orientation is to the lakefront, with grills and fire pits on a sandy beach. Weekly rates from $400–500.

Lake View Resort (906-493-5241; www.drummondislandlake view.com), 32033 E. Tourist Rd. This resort offers eight modern cottages with a view of Potagannissing Bay. All offer kitchens. The family-style resort is run by Steve and Karen Kemppainen. Weekly rates from $440.

IN GRAND MARAIS (PICTURED ROCKS, HIAWATHA WATER TRAIL)

Hilltop Cabins and Motel (906-494-2331), N. 14176 Ellen St., near CR H58, about 0.5 mile east of the center of Grand Marais. With a mix of housekeeping cabins and motels, this is the perfect spot for kayakers—especially a large group. There's plenty of room for vehicles with boats, and there's a fire pit to hang around during evening hours. The resort is owned and operated by John and Jeanette Bauknecht and is kayak friendly. Jeanette is an avid kayaker and is a good source of information about local conditions. Most of the rooms have been remodeled and there are impressive, newer large cabins. There are no phones in the rooms, but they offer wireless Internet access. Rates from $75–200.

Sunset Cabins (906-494-2693), off CR H58 on Lake Superior, east of Grand Marais. With beach access, this would be a perfect place to stay and launch your boat from for day trips around Grand Marais Harbor and along the Lake Superior shoreline. The cabins are quintessential Up North places, most handcrafted by owner Craig Winnie. It's in a quiet location. Call for reservations, because many folks book the same places year after year; there are often no vacancies. Rates from $100–125 per night, $670–760 weekly.

North Shore Lodge (906-492-2361), 22020 Coast Guard Pt., Grand Marais. Located at the tip of the point, this lodge is ideal for a paddling vacation and has lakefront access to Grand Marais Harbor and Lake Superior. The lodge is the most complete resort in the area and offers 42 traditional motel rooms and housekeeping cabins. There's a full-service restaurant and bar offering breakfast, lunch, and dinner. There's an indoor pool, sauna, and hot tub. Rates from $90–110.

IN MUNISING (PICTURED ROCKS, HIAWATHA WATER TRAIL, INDIAN RIVER)

Alger Falls Cottage (906-387-3536; www.algerfallsmotel.com), E. 9427 MI 28, Munising. The two-bedroom cabin near the Pictured Rocks National Lakeshore sleeps up to six people and has a fully equipped kitchen, dining area, and comfortable living area. The bath has a tub and shower. There is an adjoining motel, but the cottage is nested in the woods and away from the comings and goings at the motel. It's close to Alger Falls and near snowmobile trails. Rates from $47–68.

Terrace Motel (906-387-2754), 420 Prospect St., Munising. This 18-room motel is two blocks from MI 28, the major artery, and offers a quiet place. There is a sauna and an indoor repair area for snowmobiles. Rates from $36–55.

Sunset Motel on the Bay (906-387-4574), 1315 Bay St., Munising. Basic motel units with a view of Lake Superior and beach access. This is just the place for paddlers who want to launch from their doorstep. Some rooms have knotty pine paneling and refrigerators and microwaves. Rates from $50–60.

IN BIG BAY (HIAWATHA WATER TRAIL, INDEPENDENCE LAKE)

Thunder Bay Inn (906-345-9376; www.thunderbayinn.net), 400 Bensinger Rd. This inn, opened in 1910 by lumber barons, was used as a warehouse, general store, office, and barbershop until 1917—when the Brunswick Co. turned it into a company store and added rooms on the second floor for loggers. In 1940 it was bought by Henry Ford, who had it renovated to serve as a retreat for himself and his executives. It fell on hard times during the 1970s, but was purchased and renovated in the mid-1980s. These days, it's called a bed & breakfast inn. It has 12 rooms, all with baths (see *Eating Out*). Rates from $76–130.

Big Bay Point Lighthouse Bed & Breakfast (906-345-9957; www.bigbaylightouse.com), #3 Lighthouse Rd., Big Bay. Perched on the rocky shore of Lake Superior, this B&B is a great place to get away from the world. The seven-room inn opened in 1986. While the rooms have baths, they don't have TV or phones. There is a common living room, library, and sauna. The lighthouse is on a secluded 40-acre parcel, which offers hiking trails. There are fireplaces in some rooms. If you're looking for more space, try the keeper rooms. The Northern Lights can be seen throughout the summer. Rates from $106–187.

Big Bay Depot Motel (906-345-9350), on Lake Independence, CR 550. This motel offers a bonus for Big Bay—five rooms with kitchens. Eating options are scarce, limited to two tavern/restaurants and a small breakfast and lunch spot. Cram's General Store, which offers groceries, is nearby. The rooms are clean and have an old-cabin feel. There is a small dock on the lake and a good view of the water. Rates from $50–60.

IN MARQUETTE (HIAWATHA WATER TRAIL)

The Landmark Inn (906-228-2580 or 1-888-752-6362; www.theland markinn.com), 230 N. Front St., Marquette. This elegant 62-room hotel is a real find in the UP, especially after a few days of paddling. It's one of only a few UP hotels with a decent lobby, and it also boasts a penthouse cocktail lounge with a view of Lake Superior. The hotel opened in the 1930s, but by the early 1980s it was in decline and it closed in 1982. It was restored and reopened in 1997. Rates from $125–269.

Blueberry Ridge B&B (906-249-9246), 18 Oakridge Dr. This traditional B&B has three rooms and is furnished with comfortable homemade quilts and antiques. There is a large stone fireplace, and breakfast is served on fine china. Rates are $100.

Johnson's Cottage on the Bay (906-228-4569), 525 Erie Ave. This two-bedroom cottage is a great place for a family to stay, with queen beds and air mattresses for the kids. The kitchen is fully equipped and there's a deck and outdoor grill. It's not fancy and the décor is decidedly cottage, but it's a good alternative to a motel room. Rates $150 daily, $875 weekly.

Cedar Motor Inn (906-228-2280 or 1-888-551-7378), 2523 US 41 W., Marquette. This 43-room motel on the outskirts of Marquette is just the place to reorganize after camping. It has cable TV and wireless Internet access so you can check your e-mail. There are even housekeeping rooms with refrigerators and microwaves for snowmobilers and anglers with longer stays. Rates are $50.

IN ISHPEMING/NEGAUNEE (HIAWATHA WATER TRAIL)

Negaunee Union Station Depot Lodge (906-475-7939; www.union stationdepot.com), 212 Gold St., Negaunee. This historic railroad depot, built in 1910, has been renovated into lodging for travelers and can hold up to eight guests. The facility has kitchen service and can be rented by large groups. Rates from $150–175.

Jasper Ridge Inn (906-485-2378), 1000 River Pkwy. This newer hotel offers a variety of rooms, including whirlpool suites, and is adjacent to the Jasper Ridge Restaurant. The inn offers clean basic rooms for travelers. Snowmobilers can park their machines here and also ride into the surrounding area. This isn't the type of inn with a lot of atmosphere; it's a basic hotel. The focus here is on outdoor activities, and this is just a place to crash after a hard day outside. Rates from $60–100.

Wonderland Motel (906-485-1044), 873 Palms Ave., Ishpeming. A mom-and-pop motel, it offers 11 rooms and a free continental breakfast. Although the rooms are small, it's a roof over your head and a hot shower. Rates from $50–60.

IN GERMFASK (FOX/MANISTIQUE RIVERS)

Northland Outfitters (906-586-9801; www.northoutfitters.com), MI 77, Germfask. There are five log-style cabins, some housing six to eight people. The bath is up the path and there are no kitchens—but they have microwaves, coffeemakers, and cable TV. There's also a campground on the property. A family-run resort, they also offer canoe /kayak rental, camping equipment, and trip planning.

    Jolly Roger Motel (906-586-6385), 8007 MI 77, Germfask. Basic motel rooms. Prices from $65–75.

IN SENEY (FOX/MANISTIQUE RIVERS)

Fox River Motel (906-499-3332; www.foxrivermotel.com), corner of MI 28 and MI 77, Seney. Clean, newer motel rooms, several with kitchens. Rates from $75–100.

IN AU TRAIN (AU TRAIN AND INDIAN RIVERS)

Au Train River Cabin (906-892-8367; www.exploringthenorth.com /autrainriver/cabin), N. 7163 Forest Lake Rd., Au Train. The cabin sleeps up to six and has a fully equipped kitchen, deck, and grill. Rates are $150 daily.

    Au Train River Lodge (906-892-8367; www.exploringthenorth .com/autrainriver/lodge), E. 5449 Curtis Dr., Au Train. The lodge overlooks the river, sleeps six to ten, and has a fully equipped kitchen and a hot tub. Rates are $200 daily.

Eating Out

IN HESSEL/CEDARVILLE (LES CHENEAUX ISLANDS)

Hessel Bay Inn (906-484-2460), 186 Pickford Ave. Open daily for breakfast, lunch, and dinner. It's the locals' hangout for casual dining inside or on the deck. The menu runs from sandwiches to steak and seafood. Prices from $5–20.

    AngGio's Restaurant (906-484-2435), MI 134, Cedarville. This is the place for a hearty breakfast before a day on the water. It's open daily, and is a favorite of the locals. Prices from $8–15.

Snows Bar & Grill (906-484-1203), across from the Snows Channel, 1187 Park Ave. on 4-mile block in Cedarville. Open May through September for lunch and dinner. The menu starts with pub food and works its way up to full dinners with soup and salad. Much of the whitefish and perch offered are locally caught. The classic pine-paneled tavern is a favorite of island residents who bring their boats over for a night on the town. Prices from $8–20.

ON DRUMMOND ISLAND (LAKE HURON)

Bayside Dining (906-493-5480), Maxton and Tourist Rds. Open late May to September, and weekends the rest of the year. Located at Drummond Island Resort, this full-service restaurant is your best bet on the island and offers whitefish, pasta, pork loin, and steaks. Prices from $15–30.

Chuck's Place (906-493-5480), Johnswood Rd., 6 miles east of Four Corners. Open daily. This classic North Woods tavern is where the locals hang their hats. Prices from $8–15.

IN PARADISE (TAHQUAMENON RIVER)

Tahquamenon Falls Brewery & Pub (906-492-3300), located on MI 123 near the entrance to Tahquamenon State Park. Owner Lark Carlye Ludlow has put together a brewpub/restaurant in an area that usually doesn't support such upscale establishments. You won't find anything like it within 25 miles. Steak and whitefish are top items, along with pub-food standards such as buffalo burgers. Prices from $15–25.

Yukon Inn (906-492-3264), 8347 N. MI 123. Open daily. It's a classic Up North knotty-pine family-style tavern that serves pub food. Prices from $8–12.

Little Falls Inn Red Flannel (906-492-3529), 8112 N. MI 123. This is one of the few places in Paradise where you can get a full dinner with a salad. Entrees are steak and whitefish. Prices from $8–15.

IN GRAND MARAIS (PICTURED ROCKS, HIAWATHA WATER TRAIL)

Lake Superior Brewing Co. (906-494-2337), 14283 Lake Ave., Grand Marais. Open daily. This traditional North Woods brewpub is filled with animal mounts and examples of cut agate rocks from the Lake Superior beaches. The brewpub is the source of handcrafted beer (try the Puddingstone Light) and burgers and pizza—and also local information. The menu occasionally moves above tavern fare, and whitefish, steak, and chicken dinners are offered. The tavern was called the Dunes Saloon for many years and many people still refer to it by that name. Prices from $10–15.

North Shore Lodge (906-494-2361; www.exploringthenorth .com/welkers/resort), 22020 Coast Guard Pt. Open mid-May through mid-March. This is the closest thing Grand Marais has to a full-service eating establishment, and it's the only place in town offering breakfast, lunch, and dinner. The crowd is mostly made up of tourists staying at the motel/cabin resort (see *Lodging*). The fare is fairly standard for breakfast and lunch, but in the evenings try the whitefish if it's on the menu. There is still one commercial fisherman plying his trade in the area, and his fresh fish is often offered. Prices from $10–15.

West Bay Diner (906-494-2647), Veteran Ave., Grand Marais. Open daily for breakfast and lunch. The restored diner is one of the few places for breakfast in town, and features home-baked breads and rolls and skillet-style breakfast dishes. Prices from $5–8.

The Bay Shore Market, (906-494-2581), Lake Ave. Open 7 AM–11 PM. Offers basic items such as meat, vegetables, canned goods—and beer, wine, and liquor. The wine selection in the UP can be thin, but the market does offer a few decent wines with a cork. Don't laugh—some don't. It also carries charcoal for grills.

IN MUNISING (PICTURED ROCKS, GRAND ISLAND)

The Navigator (906-387-1555), 101 E. Munising Ave. Open daily. This family-style restaurant serves breakfast, lunch, and dinner. There are homemade soups and full meals, with daily specials including whitefish and steak. It's close to the dock for the Pictured Rocks boat tours. Prices from $8–12.

Dogpatch (906-387-9948; www.dogpatch.com). Open daily. If you can get past the name, this is a decent restaurant for this area, serving fish, steaks, chicken, pizza, burgers, and a breakfast buffet. You're going to find more on the menu here than at most places in this area. Prices from $8–15.

IN BIG BAY (HIAWATHA WATER TRAIL, INDEPENDENCE LAKE)

Thunder Bay Inn (906-345-9376; www.thunderbayinn.net), 400 Bensinger Rd. Open daily. The movie *Anatomy of a Murder* was filmed here in 1959, and it has been a cottage industry ever since. Sandwiches on the menu are named for characters in the movie, and the restaurant was ordered built by Otto Preminger, the director, because the regular dining room didn't look enough like a North Woods bar. There is pizza, steak, and whitefish. Prices from $6–10 (see *Lodging*).

   Cram's General Store (906-345-0075; www.cramsgeneralstore .com), CR 550. Open daily. If you go to Big Bay, you'll find yourself at Cram's, which is the only gas station and grocery store in town. Owners Joe and Kathy Cram operate this old-time country store, which offers bread, milk, meat, produce, and beverages—along with local information. Coffee is in a Styrofoam cup—but it's hot, and this is one of the few places in town to get a cup in the morning. The store also offers an ATM machine, hunting and fishing licenses, movie rentals, auto parts, and a fax machine. There is also a selection of hardware and camping gear. If they don't have it, chances are you'll be driving to Marquette.

   Hungry Hollow Café is adjacent to the general store and serves breakfast and lunch, but is closed at dinnertime. This is a basic ham-and-egg breakfast place, but most folks in town end up here because it's the only place in Big Bay to offer a full breakfast menu. Lunch brings burgers, soup, and sandwiches. Don't expect anything fancy. Prices from $5–7.

IN MARQUETTE (HIAWATHA WATER TRAIL)

Vierling Restaurant & Marquette Harbor Brewery (906-228-3533; www.thevierling.com), 119 S. Front St. This brewpub offers pub food, but also fine dining in a casual atmosphere in a historic building. There has been a saloon/restaurant at this site for more than 100 years. The building received a facelift in the mid-1980s when its current owners, Kristi and Terry Doyle, took over—but it still has an 1890s feel. The beer is made on-site. The red ales were excellent, and there is a decent wine list. The local whitefish dishes are a real find after a day of UP road

A loaded canoe during an extended day tour along the shoreline

food, which typically consists of burgers and pizza. Prices from $12–20.

The Sweetwater Café (906-226-7009; www.sweetwatercafe.org), 517 N. 3rd St.. Open daily, 8 AM–8 PM. This place has all the bases covered with its bakery, restaurant, and bar. Breakfast here is a treat, with its freshly baked bread and other baked goods. The French toast is a great bet in the morning. Lunches with homemade soup, salads, and sandwiches are a welcome respite after a morning on the road. There is a small bar area, but it's not the type of place you'd want to spend an evening.

IN ISHPEMING/NEGAUNEE (HIAWATHA WATER TRAIL)

Congress Pizza (906-486-4233), 106 N. Main St., Ishpeming. Open daily. This tavern/restaurant is a local hangout for Ishpeming, and has a long history of serving up brick-oven baked pizza. The menu is limited to pizza, *cudighi* sandwiches, and pizza fries. Cudighi is a locally made Italian sausage flavored with nutmeg. They don't even have it in Italy, my server told me. It's a tangy, spicy sausage and well worth trying. The tavern's history reflects that of Ishpeming. It was founded in 1934 by A. Louis Bonetti, an Italian immigrant, who came to work in the area iron mines and opened the tavern after the repeal of Prohibition, naming it for the U.S. Congress because it had voted to end Prohibition. Prices from $5–10.

IN CURTIS (FOX/MANISTIQUE RIVERS)

Chamberlin's Ole Forest Inn (906-586-6000; www.chamberlinsinn
.com), N. 9450 County Rd., Curtis. You don't expect to find such fine
dining in this neck of the woods. Folks come from around the region
for a night at this old lumberman's hotel that now serves as a restaurant
and bed & breakfast. On the menu are fish, pasta, chicken, steaks, and
pork. There is also a fine wine cellar. There's a pub where sandwiches
and burgers are served. Dining room prices from $16–25, pub prices
from $8–10.

IN SENEY (FOX/MANISTIQUE RIVERS)

Andy's Seney Bar (906-499-3382), MI 28. This is a sportsman's-style
tavern that serves up pub food and beer. Prices from $6–8.

NEAR AU TRAIN (HIAWATHA WATER TRAIL, AU TRAIN
AND INDIAN RIVERS)

Brownstone Inn (906-892-8332; www.brownstoneinn.com), MI 28, 2
miles west of the Au Train blinking light. This historic stone building
dating from 1946 and made mostly of local materials is a real find in
this area, with a full service dinner menu that includes steak, chicken,
seafood, and fish. Prices from $10–20.

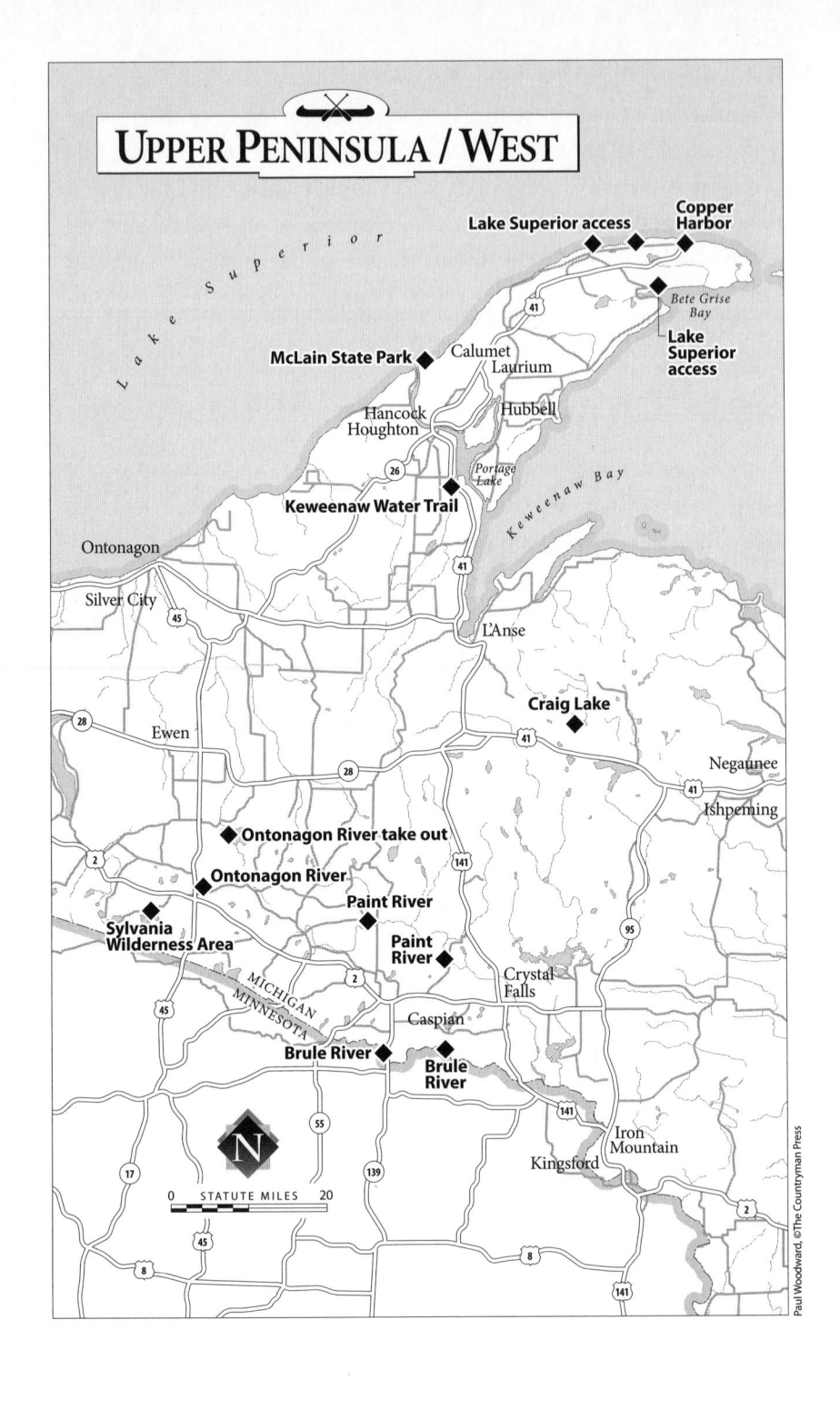

Part 5—Western Upper Peninsula

Keweenaw Peninsula, Isle Royale National Park, Craig Lake, Paint River, Brule River, Sylvania Wilderness and Recreation Area, Ontonagon River

FROM THE ROCKY coast line of the Keweenaw Peninsula along Lake Superior to the vast Sylvania Lakes, the western UP offers sea kayaking, inland lake paddling, and wilderness travel by canoe or kayak.

While many head further northwest to the Boundary Waters, Michigan has its own version—Sylvania Lakes and Craig Lake State Park—where you can travel for weeks by canoe or kayak.

The region is sparsely populated and there are few canoe/kayak liveries, and even fewer services available to move your vehicle from put-in to take-out, so planning is very important. Having an off-the-road vehicle (ORV) or a mountain bike would help you plan a float on a remote river.

Also, apart from a few larger towns like Iron Mountain, Escanaba, and Ironwood, paddlers will find few places to pick up extra pieces of needed gear, so make sure to remember everything when traveling to this region.

42. Keweenaw Peninsula

Best Runs: Keweenaw Water Trail (around the tip of the Keweenaw), about 100 miles, 6–8 days
Accessibility: Excellent
Skill Level: Intermediate to advanced (beginners if with an outfitter)
Best Times: Late May to Sept.
Description: Lake Superior waters are clear and cold, about 40–50 degrees in the summer
Home Base: Copper Harbor or Houghton/Hancock
Location: Western UP, north of MI 28 on MI 41

IF PADDLERS HAVE only one choice of a Lake Superior paddling destination, this should be it. The Keweenaw Peninsula Water Trail offers more than 100 miles of rugged coastline and cliffs, protected harbors and bays, and exposed shorelines to paddle. The adventurous can

Lake Superior shows its rough side to kayakers

make the trip to Manitou Island on the northeastern tip of the peninsula.

The trip around the peninsula allows paddlers to put in at one place and take out at the same spot. The paddle takes six to eight days, and possibly longer if the weather kicks up. There are developed and primitive campsites along the shoreline, and there are also small resort towns that offer lodging and dining possibilities. Most of the shoreline is either owned by the state of Michigan or is in the hands of land trusts, which allow public use of the property. The basic rule is—if it's posted, it's private.

A kayak sits on the shores of the Keweenaw Peninsula

If you're planning a trip around the entire peninsula, go to www.kwta.org for a detailed, waterproof map with marked campgrounds and other features along the way.

For paddlers looking for recreational day paddles, the possibilities are endless. A good home base for those taking day trips is Copper Harbor, which offers a diversity of lodging in small motels, larger lodges, cabins, and camping. There are also decent restaurants there, and also in nearby Eagle Harbor.

Copper Harbor also offers attractions, if the weather keeps paddlers off the lake for a day or two. Copper Harbor was developed in the 1840s by copper miners who came to seek their fortunes. It was akin to the California Gold Rush, and the federal government soon established Fort Wilkins—and its soldiers were charged with keeping order among the miners who were seeking to stake claims to mines. The fort is now a state park, and it has been restored.

The copper discovery sparked the settlement of the Keweenaw Peninsula, despite its harsh winters. The U.S. Park Service administers a nearly 100-square-mile historic park that stretches from Houghton/ Hancock to Calumet, and includes old mines and buildings.

The peninsula is dotted with many near ghost towns—including Delaware, Phoenix, Mohawk, and Ahmeek—all the sites of now long- abandoned copper mines. There are also numerous cemeteries near many of these towns with the graves of miners who often died young many miles from their homelands in Wales, Sweden, Finland, or Germany.

Bete Grise Bay

Local legend has it that its French name means gray beast and it comes to us via a Native American legend that a young Indian woman lost her man in the bay to a gray beast. That meaning has morphed in recent times in the mouths of paddlers to mean a foggy bay, and it was like that the day I paddled it—so you get no argument from me. Its rocky shores and sandy beaches would be well worth an entire day. There's

Taking in Copper Harbor, part of Lake Superior

also a lighthouse and the mouth of Lac Labelle to see. Paddlers could also explore Lac LaBelle, which empties into the bay.

Copper Harbor

Paddlers could spend an entire day exploring the rocky shoreline and outer islands. The put-in is at the Copper Harbor Marina, which is lightly used by powerboats. Follow the shoreline to the west and then out toward where the harbor opens up into the open lake. There are some delightful rocky islands to paddle between. Depending on the weather and your skills, cross over toward the mainland for a look at Copper Harbor from the water. There isn't much powerboat traffic, but at about 7 PM the boat servicing Isle Royale pulls in and docks. Follow the coastline east to the Copper Harbor Lighthouse, which is open to the public.

Eagle Harbor

Put in at the public beach along MI 26 for a few hours or a full day. When I paddled it in late June, a foggy mist settled in and I was glad I'd brought my compass to keep my bearings. The mainland shore is sandy, but it turns rocky as it bends around the harbor.

43. Isle Royale National Park

> **Best Runs:** Day tours around Rock Harbor Lodge
> **Accessibility:** Good
> **Skill Level:** Beginner to expert
> **Best Times:** Early June to early Sept
> **Description:** Coves and harbors around the island in Lake Superior and inland lakes
> **Home Base:** Copper Harbor, Houghton, and Grand Portage, Minnesota
> **Location:** Western UP off Keweenaw Peninsula

SITTING ABOUT 50 MILES northwest of the Keweenaw Peninsula in Lake Superior, Isle Royale National Park has long been a destination for backpackers, boaters, and paddlers. It's not a casual destination, and paddlers have to make a real time commitment to visit the park. The boat ride from the mainland is four to six hours, and there's a fee to transport a canoe or kayak.

There are no roads on the island, and travel is restricted to boats or on foot. Greenstone Ridge is the rocky backbone of the island, running its length. On clear days you can see the 15 miles to Canada from it.

The island hasn't always been a wilderness. Native Americas were mining copper there as early as 2000 BC, and Europeans followed in the early 19th century. The most extensive operation still visible is at Mc-Cargo Cove, which once supported a small village. Excavation sites can still be seen, and the park service offers guided historical tours. Commercial fishing was also conducted, and one fishery can be toured.

The island supports moose and wolves, but there are no deer or black bear. Beaver are numerous in the wetlands, and red foxes abound. Many of them show up at campsites begging for food. The park service frowns on feeding them, because they become too dependent on humans and they end up starving during winter when folks aren't around.

Before you try this trip, figure out what you want to do. Expert sea kayakers may want to try circumnavigating the nearly 48-mile-long island, while others may opt to explore Moskey Basin and Todd Harbor, which are near the island's only hotel—the Rock Harbor Lodge.

Paddling out into one of the island's protected inlets

If you're a casual paddler who wants to spend a few hours exploring the rocky outer islands near Rock Harbor, you can opt to rent a canoe on the island—and not go through the expense of bringing your boat over.

For paddlers, the island has a split personality. Travel along the exposed shorelines requires a good sea kayak, while travel to interior lakes is a better task for canoes.

There are also various opportunities for mixed paddling/ backpacking trips. Several years ago my sons, a friend, and I did one. We brought my canoe over on the boat from Copper Harbor, and arrived in Rock Harbor shortly after noon. We loaded the heavy gear into the canoe, which was paddled by me and a friend. This allowed my sons, who were hiking, to travel light and make time. Often when the boat arrives, backpackers make a race for Daisy Farm Campground, about a half day from Rock Harbor, and it gets crowded early in the day. We found a campground on an outer island, and I ferried my sons there for the evening.

The campground was mostly populated with anglers in powerboats. They were great. They shared their catch of the day, lake trout, with us.

From there, we headed to Moskey Basin where my friend and I spent several nights while my sons explored the interior of the island. I've been to the island about six times, and I think Moskey Basin is the best campground on the island. There are Adirondack-style wooden shelters, each with a picnic table. Most sites are secluded and have a view of the water.

Try sticking to established campgrounds, if possible. Isle Royale is a series of rocky ridges and wetlands. The established campgrounds are on the only level ground there is. Also, don't count on getting a shelter each night, so bring a tent.

Moskey Basin attracts a lot of canoeists who are planning to portage their boats the 2.2 miles inland to Lake Richie. From there it's a 0.5 mile portage to Siskiwit Lake, the largest inland lake on the island.

One tip: Walk part of the portage from Moskey Basin to Lake Richie before committing to portaging. Over the years I've met some pretty miserable people on the trail. Summers can be hot on the island, sometimes with temperatures in the 90s—add a ton of mosquitoes to the mix, and you've got a tough haul. There are rewards, though—once in Lake Richie, you'll hardly see another soul for days.

Sea Kayaking

It's world class, but this isn't the place for a beginner unless you're with a large group and on a trip with an outfitter. Several outfitters offer kayaking tours of the island, and such trips are well worth looking into.

If you're an expert, have at it. A circumnavigation of the island would be a memorable trip. But even for experts, danger lurks—especially on the island's north shore, nearly all of which is exposed coastline and subject to strong northerly winds. However, the shoreline is fairly forgiving, although rocky, and landings can be made in most places.

I've been going to the island since the 1960s and have noticed a psychological need among backpackers and paddlers to hike the length of the island or circumnavigate it. For years, I succumbed to the same thinking—but in recent years, I've abandoned that mindset, and now am content to explore the east end of the island.

For paddlers, there are more than enough places to explore on or near Rock Harbor, Moskey Basin, and nearby Todd Harbor. There are more than a dozen outer islands to explore in the vicinity. For those arriving from Grand Portage, Minnesota, at Windigo, Grace Harbor and its outer islands are well worth exploring.

*Reflecting on the rocky
(but forgiving) area shore*

The moose/wolf population is a top island attraction. The balance of nature is intact, with the wolves and moose dependent on each other, the prey and predator. When the moose population gets too large for the habitat, the weaker ones soon become prey for the wolf packs, and the number of wolves increases. When the number of moose starts declining, food becomes more abundant and their numbers increase.

Paddling the shorelines and outer islands is the best way to see moose, which often swim from island to island to feed. It's tempting to get close, but keep a good distance away. As for wolves, listen for them at night—you rarely see them.

For those who aren't up for sleeping on the ground in a tent or shelter, Rock Harbor Lodge

Moose (swimming or eating) are easily seen from canoes or kayaks

offers rooms and a restaurant. Lesser known are the 20 cottages it rents in the Rock Harbor/Tobin Harbor vicinity. The cottages come with kitchens (see *Lodging*).

For recreational kayakers, Tobin Harbor should be at the top of their list. It's a short portage from Rock Harbor and is narrow, and well protected from the north and south winds.

Canoeists and kayakers can design trips based on being dropped off and picked up at certain points of the island by the Wenonah, which serves as a water taxi around the island (see *Voyageur II* under *Access*).

Access

Boats run from Copper Harbor, Houghton/Hancock, and Grand Portage, Minnesota.

Isle Royale Queen (906-289-4437; www.isleroyal.com), Copper Harbor. From mid-May through late July, the ferry runs on limited days. There are trips daily during August, and in September the boat returns to a limited schedule. The boat departs Copper Harbor at 8 AM and the trip takes three hours. The return trip departs from Isle Royale at 2:45 PM. Here is the schedule: Mid-May through early June, Monday and Friday; early June through mid-June, Monday, Wednesday, Friday, and Saturday; mid-June through late June, Monday, Tuesday, Thursday,

Friday, and Saturday; July, Monday, Tuesday, Thursday, Friday, Saturday, and Sunday; August, daily trips; early September, Monday, Tuesday, Thursday, Friday, Saturday, and Sunday; remainder of September, Monday and Friday. Fares are $130 per person mid-July through mid-August, early and late season fares are $114. There is a $50 fee to transport canoes/kayaks, and $60 for double kayaks.

Ranger III (906-482-8753; www.nps.gov/isro/index), 800 East Lakeshore Dr., Houghton. Trips run from early June through mid-September. Schedule: Tuesdays and Fridays, 9 AM, the boat departs Houghton for Rock Harbor; return trip, 9 AM Wednesdays and Saturdays. Low season rates, early and late summer, $100 round trip; high season rates, early July through late August, $120. Canoes/kayaks under 20 feet, $20; larger, $50.

Voyageur II (Nov.–Apr., 651-653-5872; May–Oct., 218-475-0074: www.isleroyaleboats.com), Grand Portage, Minn. This boat service provides transportation to the island and to various points around the island. It's basically also the water taxi service, and paddlers can arrange to have themselves and their boats picked up and transported around the island. Call for more details. The boat runs from mid-May through September, and leaves Grand Portage on Monday, Wednesday, and Saturday. Round-trip rates are $66 and up, depending on where you want to be dropped off. Canoes/kayaks, $64 round trip.

44. Craig Lake

> **Best Runs:** Day trips on Craig Lake
> **Accessibility:** Difficult, long portage
> **Skill Level:** Beginner to intermediate
> **Best Times:** Mid-May to Sept.
> **Description:** Chain of lakes in wilderness area
> **Home Base:** L'Anse, Ishpeming
> **Location:** Western UP, eastern Baraga County, north of MI 28

CRAIG LAKE STATE PARK is the most remote park of the state system—at the end of 7 miles of bad road, which keeps many away, including those with campers and RVs. During dry summer months an average car can make the trip—but when wet, the road can only be negotiated with a four-wheel-drive vehicle.

The park is a legacy of Milwaukee beer baron Fred Miller of Miller Brewing, an avid outdoorsman who purchased several thousand acres in the early 1950s and named lakes for his sons, Craig and Teddy, and his daughter, Claire. He built two cabins, a three-bedroom lodge, and a six-bunk cabin for his caretaker. Those cabins are still standing and can be rented from the state. Unfortunately, Miller died in a plane crash in 1954 and the land was sold to a UP logging company, which in turn sold it to the state in 1966.

The quiet waters of an Upper Peninsula lake

The more than 6,900-acre park has six lakes, and is virtually undeveloped except for the cabins and trail system. The North Country Trail which links the Adirondack Mountains with the Missouri River in North Dakota runs through the park.

Craig Lake is 374 acres and has six islands to explore, along with high granite bluffs. There are difficult portages to Claire and Crooked lakes, both about 0.5 mile over rugged terrain. Anglers willing to do the work are often rewarded with trophy-size fish—including bass, pike, and walleye. The portage from the parking lot to Craig Lake is about 0.5 mile.

If you're not up for a portage, Keewaydin Lake in the park has a boat ramp and loading dock, but you'll be sharing paddling waters with motorboats. It's the only lake on the property that allows powerboats.

Camping is allowed, but there are no designated campgrounds. There's a fee, and camps must be 150 feet from the water. This is black bear country, which means don't feed the bears or cook in your tent. Food items should be hung from a rope 25–30 feet above ground and 100 feet from your camp.

Resources

Craig Lake State Park (906-339-4461; www.dnr.state.mi.us/parksand trails/), north of MI 28, eastern Baraga County, look for brown state park sign. The rustic cabins, which are a 2 mile hike in from the parking lot, can be rented from the state. Rates from $60–80.

45. Paint River

Best Runs: Gibbs City to Block House
Accessibility: Fair
Skill Level: Beginner to intermediate
Best Times: Mid-May to Sept.
Description: Wide, clear, like a western trout stream
Home Base: Iron River
Location: Western UP off US 2, north of Iron River

THE RIVER FEELS LIKE something transplanted from the West to Michigan. It's up to 75 feet wide and has a stony bottom, like many western trout streams. Because of its remoteness, lack of many good access points, and lack of outfitters operating in the region, it gets little traffic.

But there are many rewards for those willing to make the effort to paddle it. It would make a good destination for a family looking for a wilderness camping experience, as there are many good formal and informal camping sites along its banks. Trout fishing can also be excellent. The paddle is a relief from Michigan's many narrow, winding rivers.

While the river is mostly family-friendly, the Upper and Lower Hemlock Rapids, just south of where the Hemlock River enters the Paint, can be dangerous—and are a Class III rapids that should only be run by white-water experts. There is a portage around them. Check out the Brule River nearby if you're looking for a multiday family trip, it may better suit your needs. The Brule, Paint, and Michigamme rivers

On the quiet waters of the Paint

are part of the same river system that eventually becomes the Menominee, which forms the border between Michigan and Wisconsin.

One word of caution on driving in this area: many of the backcountry roads have been renumbered in recent years, and you may get disoriented if you're not using an up-to-date set of county maps or have a GPS.

Gibbs City to Block House (5 miles, 2–3 hours): An easy first-day float

Don't look for a town when looking for Gibbs City. It's really somebody's idea of a joke. Take County Road 657 (CR 657) north off of US 2, just west of Iron River. Launch at the U.S. Forest Service campgrounds. The short paddle would make for a good shakedown cruise for a family making a multiday river trip.

As I've suggested before, I'd set up a camp beforehand at the Block House campground, and paddle to it on the first day. This way there's little gear in the canoe to get wet if there are paddling mishaps. The water is fairly fast, dropping about 4.2 feet per mile, but the river is wide and easy to maneuver on.

Putting in for a trip on the Paint

Block House to Bates-Amasa Road Bridge (12 miles, 5–6 hours): Rapids, possible portage

Depending on your paddling skills, you may want to skip this section of the river, as there are the Upper and Lower Hemlock Rapids to run. They can be done by paddlers with intermediate to expert skills, but can be easily gotten around by either portaging or hand-lining your watercraft while walking the riverbank. Make sure to bring rope. The Hemlock portage is about 0.5 mile long and is on the left. Many paddlers start at the Bates-Amasa Bridge, to avoid the falls.

Bates-Amasa Bridge to Crystal Falls Power Dam (13 miles, 5–6 hours): Difficult portage

If you're looking to float this stretch of river and want to avoid the tough portage at the Crystal Falls Dam, Erickson's Landing (to the left) is a good take-out point, and several miles downstream from the bridge. The river is 75–130 feet wide along this section, and the bottom is rocky, so it's pretty much a gentle float. The water slows when approaching the power dam. The take-out is on the left, and is barely marked and brushy. The best bet is to arrange to be picked up at the dam by a vehicle—so as to avoid a long, arduous portage—and get dropped off about 1.5 miles south at the MI 69 Bridge. Cell phones usually work in and around Crystal Falls.

MI 69 to Little Bull Dam (9 miles, 3–4 hours): Backwaters, another portage

Paddlers may just want to skip this section of backwaters paddling that extends to the Little Bull Dam, and the portage around the dam. The portage is on the east shore. There's a diversion canal to the east of the dam which has access to Peavy Pond and the Michigamme River. There's good access at the dam, and many may want to end their trip here rather than run the Horserace Rapids, which are about 2 miles downstream. There is a 1.5 mile portage around the rapids, which are extremely dangerous and should only be run by expert paddlers.

46. Brule River

Best Runs: MI 89 to Pentoga Bridge
Accessibility: Fair
Skill Level: Beginner to intermediate
Best Times: Mid-May to Sept.
Description: Wide, easy paddling
Home Base: Iron River
Location: Western UP off US 2 via MI 73 or MI 189

LUCKILY I HAVE FRIENDS with a camp near here, which is what folks in the UP call a cabin in the woods, so I've spent a lot of time paddling and fishing this lovely 40-plus miles of river—much of which forms the border with Wisconsin.

There are some rapids, but they're mostly fun to run, not nerve-wracking. Much of it is 30–50 feet wide, and there are no tight turns to negotiate. While it's often paddled from the MI 73 Bridge, I'd check that portion out before floating it. Companions and I had a rough day on the river during May due to low water conditions, and we had to get out of our canoes countless times to pull them through the shallow areas. A more reliable float is from MI 189 south of Iron River to US 2 south of Crystal Falls.

This is a good area for a GPS, as roads and numbering systems don't always match up along the Wisconsin border—and since much of the land is government-owned, roads simply have a U.S. Forest Service number.

A paddler enjoys the slow waters

MI 73 Bridge to MI 189 Bridge (13 miles, 4–5 hours): Watch out for low water

I've had trouble with low water levels on this section—and that was in May, so in July and August it could be worse. The launch is at a U.S. Forest Service campground near the bridge, but a better alternative, to avoid low water, is to put in at the end of Forest Service Road 2172 (FR 2172), which is several miles downstream and on the Wisconsin side. It's accessed via WI 55/MI 73 and is off FR 2457. It's about 10 miles on those roads from the bridge. The float is over shallow water, with a stony bottom. There's a rough access point about 3 miles west of MI 189 at a washed-out bridge at the end of Brule River Road, but it's a remote site and difficult to drive to. The take-out at MI 189/WI 139 is to the right, but the access is difficult and the parking lot is more than 100 yards away.

MI 189 to Pentoga Bridge (12 miles, 5–6 hours): Deeper water, easy Class I rapids

This is where I'd start my trip; the water deepens and there's more volume when the Iron River flows into it just west of Scott's Landing, which is a decent river access point. There are some small Class I rapids below the landing, and some boulders to dodge. Intermediate paddling skills should suffice.

Pentoga Bridge to US 2 (13 miles, 5–6 hours): 2-foot drop, rapids

Launching from Carney Landing at the end of Carney Road is a good alternative, and shortens the trip to about 6.5 miles, 3–4 hours, making it a good paddle with children. It's also a good way to avoid the 2-foot drop that creates a Class II rapids about 3 miles (1 hour) downstream of Pentoga Bridge. The rapids can be run through the center, but can also be portaged.

US 2 to Brule River (4.5 miles, 2–3 hours): Rapids, poor access, not recommended

This isn't the section of the river for recreational paddlers due to Class I and II rapids about halfway between the put-in and take-out. There's also a lack of emergency take-out spots. Washburn Bridge is the only spot, and it's difficult to drive to. The Brule ends as it drains into a flowage area, and there is a public landing about 1 mile below Washburn Bridge.

47. Sylvania Wilderness and Recreation Area

Best Runs: Day trips around Clark and Crooked lakes
Accessibility: Fair, limited to launches at Clark and Crooked lakes
Skill Level: Beginner to intermediate
Best Times: Mid-May to Sept.
Description: Chain of 12 lakes, with warm water
Home Base: Watersmeet
Location: Western UP off US 2

THIS AREA IS Michigan's version of the famed Boundary Waters Canoe area, and is less than a day's drive from population centers in Chicago and the Twin Cities. The 18,327-acre wilderness area, with its 12 lakes, is attractive to families seeking a wilderness experience as well as seasoned paddlers looking for secluded lakes (if they're up to portaging). You could travel for a month in the area and not see the same place twice.

The chain of lakes is a great family camping destination

The chain of lakes is a perfect area for a canoe, which offers families stable boats for children and large carrying capacities for camping gear. There are some powerboats (electric motors only) on Crooked Lake, but all the others are restricted to paddling only.

For families, Clark and Crooked lakes offer secluded campgrounds and easy access. Boat launches for those lakes are located at parking lots. Portages to a dozen other larger lakes can range from 0.25–0.5 mile, and are not the types of trips you'd want to take small children on.

For day paddlers, both Clark and Crooked lakes would be worth a day each if you investigated the shorelines. A day paddle mixed with some hiking would be a good way to explore the area. Try paddling to the south end of Clark Lake to the portage and walk the nearly 0.5 mile to Loon Lake.

There are plenty of loons on the lakes. One evening as I paddled Clark Lake, one put on a show for me. Because I was in a quiet kayak, I drifted very close to him and snapped photos before he dove underwater. He appeared again and he and I played games for a while, me getting very close until he dove again. Just one note on birds: the islands in the lakes are off-limits because they are used by ground-nesting birds until mid-July. Loons are fairly sensitive to pressure, as they only have a few young. It's mostly the males you'll see in early summer. Their job on the lake is to distract potential predators away from the nests. There is also a wolf population in the area.

A loon sits calmly on a lake

The area is worth seeing because it offers a glimpse of old-growth woods, a rarity in a region cut by lumber companies in the 1890s and early 20th century. Ironically, it was a lumberman, Albert Johnston, who sparked the preservation of the tract. In 1895 he bought 80 acres of property on the south end of Clark Lake. At first his intention was to cut the pines, but eventually decided to spare them and build a home there.

Several other lumbermen joined with Johnston and bought the entire township. They developed hunting and fishing lodges, but not the property. Various members of the Sylvania Club owned and managed the property through the 1960s, until it eventually was purchased by the U.S. Forest

Picking a spot to camp in the wilderness area

Service—which knocked down the old lodges and restored the land to its 1890s appearance.

PORTAGE DISTANCES TO OUTER LAKES

Crooked to High	350 feet
Crooked to Corey	545 feet
Crooked to Clark	1,790 feet
Crooked to Mountain	210 feet
Mountain to East Bear	1,540 feet
West Bear to Kerr	1,550 feet
West Bear to East Bear	640 feet
High to Kerr	610 feet
Clark to Loon	1,580 feet
Glimmerglass to Hay	2,015 feet
Whitefish to Hay	2,530 feet
Whitefish to Whitefish parking	3,875 feet
Loon to Fisher	2,240 feet
Loon to Florence	1,250 feet
Loon to Deer Island Lake	1,475 feet
Deer Island to Cub	1,265 feet
Cub to Big Bateau	110 feet
Florence to Fisher	2,130 feet
Florence to Big Bateau	540 feet

Watersmeet

The town is about 3.5 miles east of the wilderness area, and offers limited accommodations and several restaurants. If you're looking for better accommodations and dining, try Land 'O' Lakes Wisconsin, about 8 miles south of Watersmeet.

Outfitters

Sylvania Outfitters (906-358-4766; www.sylvaniaoutfitters.com), US 2, 1 mile west of Watersmeet. It's the only outfitter licensed to operate in the wilderness area and offers canoe and camping equipment rentals. Even if you've got your own equipment, this place is worth a stop for maps and information about the area.

48. Ontonagon River

Best Runs: Watersmeet to Bond Falls
Accessibility: Fair
Skill Level: Beginner to intermediate
Best Times: Mid-May to Sept.
Description: Starts narrow, but widens
Home Base: Watersmeet
Location: Western UP off US 2

THE ONTONAGON IS A sprawling river system that runs from the Watersmeet area near the Michigan-Wisconsin border to its mouth on Lake Superior near the community of Ontonagon. It's composed of south and east branches, main stream, and middle branch.

The south and east branches near Rockland can be paddled, but it's difficult work and should be done by hard-core paddlers looking for a wilderness experience. Recreational paddlers will find a better experience on the middle branch between Watersmeet and Bond Falls. Some UP natives consider the trip one of the best floats in the region.

The main stream can be run for 24 miles between US 45 and Ontonagon (24 miles, 8–11 hours). The river is slow here, and there's lots of motorboat traffic as you get near Ontonagon. Paddlers will have a better experience on the middle branch.

Checking out a falls on the Ontonagon to see if it can be run

The rewards of floating the river system are in the wildlife-viewing possibilities, which include deer, black bear, bald eagles, and even an occasional wolf sighting. This is a remote region, and the riverbanks are mostly undeveloped and wild, with pine and hardwood forests.

A trip on the middle branch would be a good way to introduce friends or family to backcountry paddling trips. It's about 19 miles from Watersmeet to Bond Falls, and a full 8–9 hour paddling day, but there's a great natural camping spot in the middle of the trip, Burned Dam Campground, which is accessible by vehicle.

For those who haven't done a lot of backcountry travel, it would be easy to set up a camp ahead of time at Burned Dam (where there is a waterfall), paddle to it, spend the night, and continue on the remainder of the trip the following day.

In this way, paddlers wouldn't have to carry camping gear and extra clothing in their canoes/kayaks—and would be assured of dry sleeping bags, clothing, and hot food at night. Paddlers wouldn't be required to set up camp after a hard and possibly wet day on the river.

Watersmeet to Burned Dam (9 miles, 5–6 hours): Sharp turns, portage around falls

Paddlers with basic to intermediate skills won't have many problems with this stretch of river that emerges in Watersmeet as a 15- to 25-foot-wide river. It's too narrow to paddle it above the US 45 Bridge, where there is good parking and a formal put-in spot that is marked and easy to find. There's another put-in at Buck Lake Road Bridge, but access is difficult. There are a few homes and cabins on the banks near town, but the riverbanks are undeveloped the remainder of the way, as the river winds through the Ottawa National Forest. The hardwoods on the low hills would make it a good fall color tour paddle. Watch for the portage, on the right, around Mex-I-Min Falls—which are too dangerous to be run by most paddlers. The campgrounds are at the falls. The best way to see them is to walk a shoreline path to the streamside below them.

Burned Dam to Bond Falls (11 miles, 4–5 hours): Rapids to run, a portage

This stretch of the river requires paddlers to muster up every bit of muscle memory they have for 300–400 feet of rapids about two hours below the falls, and every bit of skill in dodging canoe-battering rocks jutting out of the riverbed. The next take-out is Interior Bridge, which has decent access. Some paddlers may want to take out here, as the remainder of the river to Bond Falls presents swift water challenges, rapids, and some logjams that may require portages or lifting the boat over the logs. Little Falls, just before entering Bond Falls Basin, may require portaging; there's a take-out before the two falls, to the right. You may just want to get out and walk the banks before trying to run them. A two-track road runs parallel to the river here, and paddlers may want to get out at any point.

In the Area

Lodging

IN COPPER HARBOR (LAKE SUPERIOR, KEWEENAW PENINSULA)

Bella Vista (1-877-888-8439; www.bellavistamotel.com), 180 Sixth St. The complex includes motel rooms and cottages, many with a view of Copper Harbor and Lake Superior. Rates from $65–95.

Keweenaw Mountain Lodge (906-289-4403; www.atthelodge

.com), US 41. The historic log lodge was constructed in the 1930s by the Civilian Conservation Corps, and is a rustic retreat where paddlers will feel at home. There are 24 cabins and motel rooms. Some cabins sleep up to six people. Rates from $99–189.

Minnetonka Resort (906-289-4449; www.minnetonkaresort.com), US 41. The resort offers basic motel rooms and cabins. The parking is good, and paddlers will have enough space to work with gear. There's also a gift shop and museum. Rates from $75–140.

IN ISLE ROYALE NATIONAL PARK

Rock Harbor Lodge (906-337-4993, summer; 1-866-644-3003, winter), Rock Harbor, Isle Royale. The stone-and-wood classic Park Service lodge building is a throwback to the 1950s when all people wanted was a clean place to stay. There are private baths. Most rooms have a view of Lake Superior. Rates from $227–252; cottages from $220–245.

IN IRON RIVER (PAINT RIVER, BRULE RIVER)

Lac O' Seasons Resort (906-265-4881 or 1-800-797-5226), 176 Stanley Lake Dr. The resort offers 14 rental units with two to four bedrooms, either on Stanley Lake or tucked into the woods. Five are log homes, and all have TV sets. They come with fully equipped kitchens. Outside there's a swimming dock in the lake and a sandy area for wading. Canoes and boats are available to guests. Rates from $50–75.

Chicaugon Lake Inn (906-265-9244; www.chicaugonlakeinn.com), 1700 CR 424. This is a big, booming, modern motel with some whirlpool suites, microwaves, TV, and free Internet. The rooms are large. It's located near Chicaugon Lake, and there's a boat launch nearby for use by guests. Rates from $50–80.

IN WATERSMEET (ONTONAGON RIVER, SYLVANIA WILDERNESS AREA)

Sylvania Wilderness Cabins (920-731-0725; www.sylvaniawilderness cabins.com), E. 21831 Crooked Lake Rd. There are five cabins located on Crooked Lake, with two to three bedrooms, and kitchens and baths in each. They can accommodate two to six persons, and come with kitchen utensils. It's suggested that you call ahead to reserve a cabin and to get exact directions, as they are located in a remote area. Rates from $50–100 daily, $570–970 weekly.

IN LAND 'O' LAKES, WISCONSIN (ONTONAGON RIVER, SYLVANIA WILDERNESS AREA)

Bel-Air Motel (715-547-3343; www.belair-motel.com), 4163 Hwy. B. The motel offers basic rooms for those looking for a deal on lodging. Rates from $60–75.

Eating Out

IN COPPER HARBOR (LAKE SUPERIOR, KEWEENAW PENINSULA)

The Mariner North (906-289-4637; www.manorth.com), 245 Gratiot St. Open for lunch and dinner. The Mariner complex offers accommodations and a bar/restaurant. This modern resort offers steak, fish, and ribs in a dining room and tavern. Prices from $10–15.

The Tamarack Inn (906-289-4522), 512 Gratiot St. This friendly little restaurant, run by Bill and Bonnie Degowski, is a real find in Copper Harbor—a place that serves three meals a day. It's a good place for a hearty breakfast before a trip to Isle Royale, as the boat dock is a block away. The soup is homemade, and there's Lake Superior whitefish and trout. Large steaks and roasted chicken are on the menu. Prices from $8–10.

IN ISLE ROYALE NATIONAL PARK

Rock Harbor Lodge Dining Room and Snack Bar. This is the only food service available on the island, and serves breakfast, lunch, and dinner. The menu is fairly limited, but includes steak, Lake Superior fish, pasta, and pork. Beer and wine are served. The snack bar offers light fare. Lodge prices from $10–25, snack bar prices from $5–7.

IN IRON RIVER (PAINT RIVER, BRULE RIVER)

Alice's (906-265-4764), 402 W. Adams. Open for dinner from Tuesday through Sunday. This is a real find in the UP. The pasta and gnocchi are made fresh daily, just the way Alice Tarsi, the owner, learned from her mother, Concetta. There is a picture of her mother outside on a sign that reads CUCINA DE MAMA (mother's cooking). The gnocchi, or potato dumplings, are topnotch. The full dinners were more than I could eat, even after a day of paddling the nearby Paint River; half portions are available. No credit cards. Prices from $10–20.

Depot Restaurant (906-265-6341), 50 Fourth Ave., MI 189. Open daily. The train dining car turned retro restaurant is aimed in the direction of lighter appetites, and it regularly delivers. The two cars are 1960s vintage Long Island commuter cars that were refurbished by owners Steve Shepich and Jo Werner to look like they were from the 1940s. Such an upscale place is difficult to find in the UP. It's a fine place for breakfast, with waffles, omelets, pancakes, and homemade bagels. Prices from $8–20.

Riverside Pizzeria (906-265-9944), 98 E. Genesee St. Open daily. This is your basic main street pizza parlor where kids are welcome and the tables are big enough for large families. It's a cozy place where you can linger with locals, who make this their hangout. The Italian sausage on the pizza was the best choice. The pizzas are large enough for a big appetite. Prices from $8–15.

IN WATERSMEET (ONTONAGON RIVER, SYLVANIA WILDERNESS AREA)

Big Mama's Grill (906-358-4601), corner of US 2 and MI 45, Watersmeet. This is where the locals start their day with a big breakfast. There are lunch and dinner specials. Open daily. Prices from $8–12.

IN LAND 'O' LAKES (ONTONAGON RIVER, SYLVANIA WILDERNESS AREA)

1938 North Restaurant and Bar (715-547-6130), 4072 Hwy. B. You have to love a place that keeps the kitchen open for you when it's closing, like this place one day when I walked in at 9 PM and needed dinner. The fare runs from pub food to steaks and fish. Prices from $8–15.

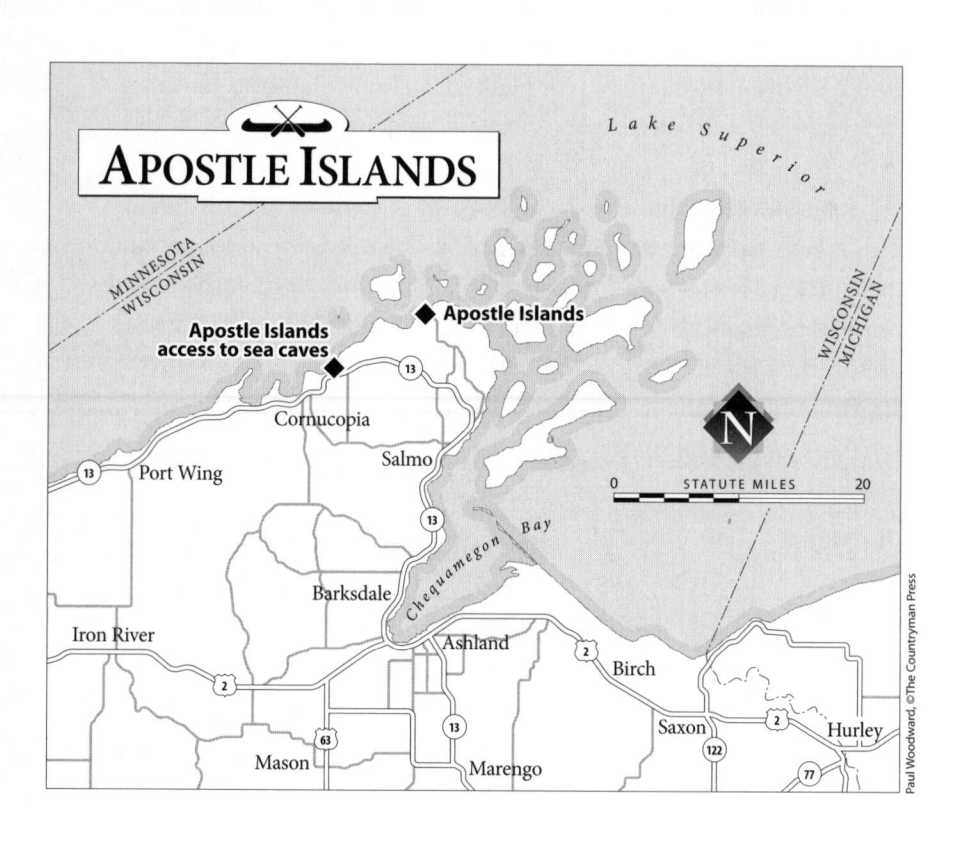

APOSTLE ISLANDS

Lake Superior

MINNESOTA
WISCONSIN

Apostle Islands
access to sea caves

◆ Apostle Islands

WISCONSIN
MICHIGAN

13

Cornucopia

13 Port Wing

Salmo

13

N

0   STATUTE MILES   20

Chequamegon Bay

13

Barksdale

Iron River

Ashland

2 Birch

2

Saxon

2 Hurley

2

63

13

122

77

Mason

Marengo

Paul Woodward, ©The Countryman Press

Wisconsin

Apostle Islands

49. Apostle Islands

Best Runs: Day to sea caves, islands
Accessibility: Somewhat difficult
Skill Level: Intermediate to expert
Best Times: Mid-May to Sept.
Description: Chain of 21 islands in Lake Superior
Home Base: Bayfield, Ashland
Location: Northern Wisconsin, north of US 2

THE APOSTLE ISLANDS in Lake Superior off the northern coast of Wisconsin are considered a top-notch paddling destination, but it's not a place for casual recreational paddlers. A trip there requires a lot of planning and advanced skills. Because of the many open-water crossings between islands, going with an outfitter is a good option.

There are some day trips along the coastline for recreational paddlers, including a trip to sea caves and an area with shipwrecks. Access is difficult, and is restricted to two sites on the west side of the Bayfield Peninsula, Meyers Beach and Little Sand Bay. Much of the shoreline is part of the Red Cliff Indian Reservation, which is considered private land.

One of the 21 islands, Madeline, is accessible via a car-carrying boat ferry, and there are two launch sites, one at La Pointe and the other at Big Bay State Park. It's the only island that's not part of the Apostle Islands National Lakeshore. Sand and Oak islands are the closest to the mainland, and the paddle is fairly easy to both, but the other islands are more difficult to reach.

A good option is to take a ferry to one of the outer islands and do some island hopping from there. Trips from Oak Island to either Manitou or Otter are only about 2 miles.

If you're determined to make the trip from the mainland for island-hopping paddling, try to be in a party of at least three to four paddlers, with one expert among the group. Sudden storms can come up and summer water temperatures of 50 degrees and less can quickly bring on hypothermia.

That said, there are many rewards—views of reddish-brown sandstone cliffs, sea caves, arches, and sea-stack rock formations among them. There are also six historic lighthouses. Wildlife abounds, and black bear can be found on all the islands.

Before striking out on your own, stop at the U.S. Park Service visitors center in Bayfield for information. There are nightly fees for camping on the islands.

Paddlers admire the sandstone cliffs of the Apostle Islands

Meyers Beach (8 miles, 4 hours): Sea cave tour

The park service maps call it a kayak launch, but there are about 50 steps down a stairway to the beach. A park ranger was on hand to help me carry my boat down, and fellow kayakers helped me on the way up. The paddle is worth the carry. The sea caves carved from sandstone start about 1 mile northeast of the launch, and you enter a world where waves meet stone. On rough days the rebounding waves make paddling difficult and potentially dangerous, but the day I was there it was fairly calm and I could paddle into them. It was like being in a stone cathedral. The winds shifted halfway into my paddle, though, so I was against the waves both ways.

Access

Apostle Islands Cruise Service (1-800-323-7619; www.apostleisland .com), City Dock, Bayfield, Wisconsin. This boat service offers tours of the islands, and transportation for kayakers traveling to the outer islands. Trip rates from $40–55, $20 per kayak.

Outfitters

Living Adventure (715-779-9503; www.livingadventure.com), off WI 13 near Red Cliff. This outfitter offers kayak lessons and trips along the shoreline and to the outer islands. Food is provided on many trips.

Trek & Trail (1-800-354-8735; www.trek-trail.com), 7 Washington Ave., Bayfield, Wisconsin. This outfitter offers day and multiple-day trips, along with boat and gear rentals. The trips are geared for everyone from beginners to those with advanced skills. There's also a photo workshop trip. They also offer cabin rentals. Cabin rates from $130–150.

Resources

Apostle Islands National Lakeshore Visitors Center (715-779-3397; www.nps.gov/apis/index), 415 Washington Ave., Bayfield, Wisconson. Information about the islands, kayaking trips, and camping fees. Open Monday to Friday in spring and fall; daily during summer. Hours 8 AM– 4:30 PM.

Little Sand Bay Visitors Center (715-779-7007; www.nps.gov/apis /index), Little Sand Bay Road, 13 miles north of Bayfield, Wisconsin.

Permits are available here, and there are exhibits. The Hokenson Brothers fishery historical site is nearby.

In the Area

Lodging

IN BAYFIELD (APOSTLE ISLAND)

Bayfield is a popular destination and it's best to make reservations.

Winfield Inn (715-779-3252; www.winefieldinn.com), 225 E. Lynde Ave., Bayfield, Wisconsin. The inn overlooks the lake and there are various lodging options to choose from, ranging from simple rooms to condos. Rates from $70–200.

Island View Inn and Cottages (715-779-5307; www.islandview bandb.com), 86720 Island View Ln., Bayfield, Wisconsin. The inn offers bed & breakfast suites and a three-bedroom cottage for larger groups. The rooms have a view of Lake Superior. Rates from $145–155.

IN ASHLAND (APOSTLE ISLANDS)

Paddlers will find more inexpensive options here, with the full array of chain motels.

Rivers Noted

I'VE INCLUDED A FEW other rivers that can be paddled, but aren't necessarily the best waters or aren't suited for recreational paddlers. Some are southern Michigan rivers that wind their ways through farmlands, others are in the UP and are difficult to paddle and have little access.

Presque Isle River

This is the toughest river to paddle in Michigan due to the numerous white-water rapids, and the lack of access in case of an emergency. Located in the northwest portion of the western UP, it offers a 20-mile trip for those with the expertise to paddle it.

The trip can be made from either Manenisco from US 2 or from MI 28, just east of Wakefield. The 14-mile trip from Marenisco to MI 28 can be made by intermediate paddlers, but from there to where the river tumbles into Porcupine Mountains State Park expert skills are needed because of the various falls and rapids. Both sections of the river are very remote and there are no canoe liveries or vehicle spotting services.

Menominee River

This river is formed near Iron Mountain when the Brule and Michigamme rivers meet. It flows nearly 100 miles to Menominee and into Lake Michigan; along the way there are one hundred tributaries and its course forms the Michigan/Wisconsin border.

However, the river isn't generally considered good for paddling, especially as the upper portion is filled with rapids and dams, and should only be considered by experts. The nearby Paint and Brule rivers are much better.

This river is included in this guide because it's home to Piers Gorge, a series of four white-water rapids that attract highly skilled paddlers from the Midwest. It's south of US 2 on MI 8 near the town of Norway. The 2.9-mile paddle's rapids are rated from Class II to IV, which for most recreational paddlers means to stay away from it.

Kayak and Canoe Resources

Kayak and canoe sales

Riverside Kayak (734-285-2925; www.riversidekayak.com), 4016 Biddle Ave. Wyandotte. The shop sells a full range of kayaks and related gear, plus it holds various demonstrations.

Kayak Corral (800-893-007; www.kayakcorral.com), 9325 W. Michigan Ave., Saline. Kayaks and related gear.

REI (www.rei.com) has three store locations in southeastern Michigan, including Northville (248-347-2100), 17559 Haggerty Rd.; Ann Arbor (734-827-1938), 970 W. Eisenhower Parkway; and Troy (248-689-4402), 766 E. Big Beaver Rd. REI offers canoes, kayaks, clothing, and paddling gear.

Dunham's Sports has 67 stores in Michigan, spread through the Upper and Lower Peninsulas, that offer canoes, kayaks, and related gear.

Summit Sports is a Michigan-based chain with several locations, including East Lansing (517-332-4000), 2650 E. Grand River Ave.; Rochester Hills (248-650-5300), 1390 Walton Blvd.; Keego Harbor (248-4444), 2867 Orchard Lake Rd.; Auburn Hills (248-364-2023), 1972 Brown Rd.; and Novi (248-468-0311), 42400 Arena Dr. All sell boats and paddling-related gear.

Bill & Paul's Sporthaus (616-458-1684; billandpauls.com), 1200 E. Paris Ave. S.E., Grand Rapids. Offers various kayaks and canoes, along with related gear.

Canoe Livery Products (231-834-5559; canoe-equipment.com), 196 S. Quarterline Rd., Scottville. Paddling and related gear.

Down Wind Sports has two Upper Peninsula locations, Marquette (906-226-7112), 514 N. Third St., and Houghton (906-482-2500), 308 Shelden Ave. Both locations offer paddling gear.

Nordic Sports (989-362-2001; n-sport.com), 218 West Bay St., East Tawas. One of the few sources of paddling gear in northeast Michigan.

The Outpost of Holland (616-396-5556; hollandoutpost.com), 25 E. Eighth St., Holland. Paddling gear and clothing.

Outfitters

Huron River

The Huron-Clinton Metro Parks (734-769-8686; www.metroparks.com). Canoe rentals are available at either Hudson Mills or Dexter and ending at Delhi Metro Park.

The livery is open daily from early June to early Sept. and only on weekends during April and from Sept. to Oct.

Skip's Huron River Canoe Livery (734-769-8686), Delhi Metro Park. Offers trips from Dexter-Huron Metro Park and Hudson Mills to Ann Arbor.

Gallop Park Canoe Livery (734-622-9319), 3000 Fuller Rd., Ann Arbor. Rents canoes and kayaks.

Heavner Canoe & Kayak (248-685-2379), 2775 Garden Rd., Milford. Offers boat rental and canoe/kayak car spotting on the upper Huron River.

Grayling (Au Sable River)

Penrod's (888-467-4837; www.penrodscanoe.com), 100 Maple St., Grayling. Canoe/kayak trips on the upper portions of the Au Sable. Vehicle spotting services.

Borchers (989-348-4921; www.canoeborchers.com), 101 Maple St., Grayling. Canoe/kayak rentals for single-day and multiple-day trips as far as the river mouth in Oscoda. Vehicle spotting services.

Carlisle Canoes (989-348-2301; www.carlislecanoes.com), 110 State St., Grayling. Rentals and trips through the river to Oscoda. Vehicle spotting services.

In Mio (Au Sable River)

Gotts' Landing (989-826-3411; www.gottslanding.com), off MI 33 at the Au Sable River, Mio. Canoe/kayak rentals, trips from Mio to Lake Huron.

Hinchman Canoe Livery (989-826-3267; www.hinchman.com), off MI 33 at the Au Sable River, Mio. Trips as far as Lake Huron, rentals of canoes/kayaks.

Roscommon (South Branch, Au Sable River)

Paddle Brave Canoe Livery & Campground (989-275-5273, www.paddlebrave.com), 10610 Steckert Bridge Rd., Roscommon. Canoe/kayak and tube rental for trips on the south branch, with shuttle service.

Hiawatha Canoe Livery (989-275-5213; www.canoehiawatha.com), 1113 Lake St., Roscommon. Canoe/kayak trips to Steckert Bridge, Chase Bridge, and from Chase to Smith Bridge.

White's Canoe Livery (989-654-2654; www.whitescanoe.com), Sterling. Offers rentals and owns several campgrounds along the river.

Sterling (Rifle River)

River View Campground & Canoe Livery (989-654-2447; www.riverviewcampground.com), 5755 N. Townline Rd., Sterling. Canoes, tubes, and kayaks for rent, along with campgrounds and cabins.

Rifle River Campground & Canoe Livery (989-654-2556; www.riflerivercampground.com), 5825 Townline Rd., Sterling. Canoe/kayak rentals, plus tubes.

Wolverine (Sturgeon River)

Henley's Canoe & Kayak (231-525-9994; www.henleysrentals.com), Wolverine City Park. Jon Henley holds forth here in a restored train depot with rental canoes, kayaks, and tubes for float trips—and good river information.

East Jordan (Jordan River)

Jordan Valley Outfitters (231-536-0006; www.jvoutfitters.com), 311 N. Lake St., East Jordan. Provides canoes/kayaks to paddlers on the Jordan River and Chain of Lakes in Antrim County.

Wellston/Irons (Pine River)

Pine River Paddlesports (231-862-3471; www.thepineriver.com), 9590 S. Grandview Hwy. S. MI 37, Wellston. Offers canoe and kayak rentals and trips, and has a campground.

Shomler Canoes and Kayaks (231-862-3475; www.shomlercanoes.com), 11390 MI 37, Irons. This livery offers trips from two hours to three days on the Pine.

Baldwin (Pere Marquette River)

Baldwin Canoe Rental (1-800-272-3642; www.baldwincanoe.com), 9117 S. M 37, Baldwin. Open from May through Oct.

Ivan's (231-745-3361; www.ivanscanoe.com), 7332 S. MI 37, Baldwin. Ivan's offers rental watercraft, a campground, and cabins.

Houghton Lake (Muskegon River)

White Birch Canoe Trips & Camping (231-328-4547; www.whitebirchcanoe.com), 4 miles west of Houghton Lake off MI 55.

River Country Campground (231-734-3808; www.campandcanoe.com), 6281 River Rd., Evart. Campgrounds and watercraft rentals.

Beaver Island (Lake Michigan)

Inland Seas School of Kayaking (231-448-2221; www.inlandseaskayaking.com), P.O. Box 437, Beaver Island, 49782. This school handles lessons for beginners through experts, and also offers day and extended trips around the island.

Honor/Glen Arbor (Platte and Crystal Rivers)

Riverside Canoe Trips (231-325-5622; www.canoemichigan.com), MI 22 at the Platte River, Honor. Offers canoe/kayak rentals for trips on the upper and lower Platte River, and a spotting service for those with their own boats.

Crystal River Outfitters (231-334-4420; www.crystalriveroutfitters.com), 6249 W. River Rd., Glen Arbor. Rents canoes, kayaks, and float tubes for 4- to 5-hour trips from Glen Lake to Lake Michigan via the Crystal River.

Hessel (Les Cheneaux Islands, Lake Huron)

Woods & Water Ecotours (906-484-4157; www.woodswaterecotours.com), 20 Pickford, Hessel. Offers kayak lessons, tours, and extended trips to the islands, nearby Drummond Island, and to Isle Royale in Lake Superior.

Paradise/Newberry (Tahquamenon River)

Tahquamenon General Store (906-492-3560; www.exploringthenorth.com/tahquagen /store), 39991 W. MI 123, Paradise. The store offers canoe/kayak rentals for 17-mile trips on the river from the Lower Falls to the river mouth at Whitefish Bay, and rental boats for use on local inland lakes. They also offer a shuttle service those who bring their own boats. The shuttle cost is $25.

The Woods, Tahquamenon River Canoe & Kayak Rental (906-203-7624; www .thewoodscanoerental.net), corner of MI 123 and Fordney Tower Rd., 13 miles north of Newberry. Open daily from mid-June through mid-Sept. No credit cards. The livery offers trips on the upper portion of the river above the falls. It also offers shuttle service for those who have their own boats.

Newberry (Two Hearted River)

Rainbow Lodge (906-658-3357; www.exploringthenorth.com/twoheart/rainbow), 32752 CR 423, Newberry. This lodge and canoe livery is located at the mouth of the Two Hearted River on Lake Superior, and it's really the only place around.

Germfast (Fox/Manistique rivers)

Northland Outfitters (906-586-9801; www.northoutfitters.com), MI 77, Germfask. Tom Kenney, the owner, is the river master here, offering trips on the Fox and Manistique rivers—and plenty of good advice. There are also cabins and campsites for rent.

Keweenaw Peninsula/Isle Royale (Lake Superior)

Keweenaw Adventure Co. (906-289-4303; www.keweenawadventure.com), 155 Gratiot St., Copper Harbor. Offers lessons, trips around the peninsula and to Isle Royale.

Watersmeet (Ontonagon River)

Sylvania Outfitters (906-358-4766; www.sylvaniaoutfitters.com), US 2, 1 mile west of Watersmeet. The only outfitter licensed to operate in the Sylvania Wilderness area; offers canoe and camping equipment rentals.

Apostle Islands (Lake Superior)

Living Adventure (715-779-9503; www.livingadventure.com), off WI 13 near Red Cliff. This outfitter offers kayak lessons and trips along the shoreline and to the outer islands. Food is provided on many trips.

Trek & Trail (1-800-354-8735; www.trek-trail.com), 7 Washington Ave., Bayfield, Wisconsin. This outfitter offers single-day and multiple-day trips along with boat and gear rentals. Trips are geared for everyone, from beginners to those with advanced skills.

Government agencies

Michigan Department of Natural Resources (www.michigan.gov/dnr). The DNR's website offers information about paddling and camping in Michigan.

The **U.S. Forest Service** (www.fs.usda.gov) manages the Huron-Manistee, Hiawatha, and Ottawa National Forests.